ENABLING EDUCATION
experiences in special and ordinary schools

This book is to be returned on or before
the last date stamped below.

ENABLING EDUCATION
experiences in special and ordinary schools

Priscilla Alderson and Christopher Goodey

the Tufnell Press,

47 Dalmeny Road,
London, N7 0DY

First published 1998

British Library Cataloguing-in-Publication Data
A catalogue record for this book is
available from the British Library

ISBN 1 872767 76 1

Printed in England by Da Costa Print, London

Contents

ACKNOWLEDGEMENTS

We are grateful to all the school students, their parents and other family members who generously took part in the interviews, to the school staff and governors, LEA staff and members who also gave interviews, to the head teachers who allowed us to observe their schools and to everyone in the schools who let us observe and talk with them, and to all the other people who contributed ideas and experiences to this project.

We would like to thank the Gatsby Charitable Foundation for sponsorship. The Calouste Gulbenkian Foundation funded a small parallel study which we refer to.

We appreciate the help of Jackie Lee, Dorothy Clift and Sarah Johnson with transcribing interview tapes, Naomi Pfeffer and Tom Shakespeare for commenting on drafts, and our colleagues who discussed our work with us.

TERMS

Ordinary schools are inclusive schools which reflect the whole ordinary society of their neighbourhood and accept any local children or teenagers. They are in contrast to *special schools* and *mainstream excluding* or *selective schools*.

Students: We use the rather clumsy terms 'pupil', 'student' and 'young people' instead of 'children' to include teenagers.

At times we use '*I*' which refers to the researcher conducting the particular observation.

Impairment usually denotes a physical or sensory problem, whereas *disability* often denotes social problems and barriers which can follow impairments. These can frequently be overcome, such as by having accessible buildings and inclusive schools.

Inclusion and *integration* are taken to mean involving impaired or disturbed students as full members of their ordinary school community. An *inclusive LEA* has a programme of encouraging inclusive schools and helping them to avoid the need to select or exclude students.

Differentiation Teaching a lesson on several levels at once, to allow for the different ability and pace of members of mixed classes.

Key stages Key stage 1 is for 5–7 year olds, 2 is for 8–10 years, 3 is for 11–13 years and 4 is for 14–16 years.

Year groups Year 1 begins at 5 years, 6 is for 10–11 year–olds,
7 for 11–12 year–olds is the first secondary school class,
year 11 for 15–16 year–olds is the final compulsory school year

The following abbreviations are used.

ASD	autistic spectrum disorder
EBD	emotional and behavioural difficulties—this variously refers to students, schools, specialist staff and policies affecting them
FE	further education college—comprehensive colleges though usually with separate 'special needs' departments
GCSEs	General Certificate of Secondary Education, exams usually for 16 year–olds
HS	high school/ secondary modern school
MLD	moderate learning difficulties
OFSTED	Office for standards in education
PD	Physical disability
PMLD	profound and multiple learning difficulties
PRU	pupil referral unit, mainly for excluded pupils
SATs	standardised attainment tests, national tests for 7, 11 and 14–year–olds
SEN	special educational needs
SENCO	special educational needs coordinator
SLD	severe learning difficulties
SpL	speech and language difficulties
VI	visual impairment

During transcripts, / denotes an interruption, and ... denotes a pause or words omitted.

Chapter 1

Setting the scene

Special education: a matter for experts or citizens?

Special education is often thought of as an expert matter, dealt with by special staff, and 'really' done in special schools (Hill, 1995). It is still mainly written about and discussed by special educationalists, the expert 'insiders'. Few studies describe daily life in special schools, or report the views of the students and their parents as this book does, or take the position of questioning 'outsiders' which, as social researchers, we have taken. Our aim is to encourage public debate by setting out the key issues plainly, for the general reader. About eighteen percent of all pupils have identified special needs, about three per cent have individual statements of special educational need, and about two per cent attend special schools, as they did fifteen years ago. One seventh of the education budget, £2.5 billion, is spent on special education (DfEE, 1997a). We are writing for ordinary citizens who are affected by special education, whether as tax payers, or students, former students or parents at special or ordinary schools. We are writing for school governors, councillors and politicians, for mainstream as well as special school staff, and for people like journalists who run news stories about impaired children, or members of voluntary organisations who raise funds for them.

The research on which this book is based

We hope to dispel some of the mystique about special education. To do so, we report the views of young people we interviewed and observed at home and school. Their experiences challenge experts' bland reports about 'consistent quality', 'significant improvements' and 'successful strategies'. The 1970s–1980s produced vivid studies of individual students and classes, (for example, Madge and Fassam, 1982; Booth et al. 1987). Such studies are now less common, with important exceptions (Wade and Moore, 1992; Cooper, 1993; Lewis 1995; Armstrong, 1995). We also set the students' experiences in their social and political context. During 1994–1996, we researched two LEAs which we call East City and West County. The comparisons cover several layers, as shown in table 1. Most of the special school literature is about layers 5, 7 and 8, the views of the experts; it seldom considers the other layers, or links between the layers, or general comparisons between special and ordinary schools, or between segregating and more inclusive LEAs.

Table 1. Layers of experience and influence which affect education

1.	Children's and teenagers' views: what do they enjoy, worry about, and hope for from their schools?
2.	Parents' experiences, hopes and fears.
3.	The home, neighbourhood, local friends, transport.
4.	Daily life at school, class and break times. Types of ordinary and special schools.
5.	Views of teachers and other staff and governors. Staff training and support.
6.	The social and political setting of the school and governors. Staff training and support.
7.	Views of LEA staff and members, LEA policies and budgets.
8.	National education policy.
9.	International policy like the United Nations Convention on the Rights of the Child 1989, and UNESCO, *The Salamanca Statement*, 1984.

We investigated the views and experiences of pupils with physical, sensory, emotional or learning difficulties, and of adults responsible for them. We observed daily activities in schools and interviewed young people, their parents and sometimes other family members, school staff and governors, and LEA members and staff (see appendix 1). When the differing views are seen together, a clearer understanding of the complex relations between them can emerge.

The two LEAs are at extreme opposite ends of the special education spectrum. In East City, most disabled children attend mainstream, mixed ability, coeducational, multi–ethnic schools. The LEA regards segregation as discriminatory and has a policy to close the special schools; only one is now still open. Unlike most 'inner city' areas, East City entirely lacks middle class housing pockets, and there is no clear consensus that some schools are better than others. West County is also exceptional, but in the amount of selective places. There are seven special schools and fifteen special units, some quite newly opened, with plans to open more, besides further special schools run by voluntary organisations. The mainstream secondary schools are grammar or high (secondary modern), almost entirely white, single sex schools, and there are twenty three private schools in the area. In West County, some primary and most secondary school uniforms signify the pupils' officially assessed ability or their parents' income.

Our report about inclusion and integration aims to respect the personal integrity of each student and the practical means of helping them to realise their potential as integrated members of their community (Booth, 1996). 'Integration' usually refers to the process of forming disparate parts (such as children) into an integral whole (such as a school), and outsiders into the mainstream. We also consider the integrity of each part, as well as the whole, in that each person feels, to some degree, accepted for himself or herself. We examine how schools attempt to balance the sometimes opposing ideals of promoting excellence yet tolerance, self–development yet altruism, and necessary special treatment yet inclusion.

Background of special education

Charitable schools for deaf and blind children opened in the eighteenth and nineteenth centuries, when large asylums or long–stay hospitals were built for mentally ill and 'subnormal' people. Like museums, the hospitals furthered the Victorian enthusiasm for classifying types, and the psychological study of mental states and abilities developed. Conditions like Down's syndrome came to be treated as illnesses requiring life–long hospital care. The building of separate schools during the 1920s for feeble–minded young people was part of wide–ranging local government programmes to improve the stock of the nation and prevent inter–breeding between different ability groups (Pailthorpe, 1932; Musgrove, 1984; Quick *et al.*, 1990).

By the 1970s, attitudes were changing, and the asylums were criticised for oppressively excluding people from ordinary life, and for misclassifying many inmates as 'abnormal' (Dobash and Dobash, 1986). Impaired children's needs for ordinary family and school life were stressed (DHSS, 1979). Long–stay hospitals were reduced in size or closed during the 1980s for financial and social reasons. Many parents, health and education professionals, and voluntary organisations like Mencap opposed hospital closures. They said closures were an excuse to cut public funding, and that expert institutional care was better than life outside in a rejecting society. The debate is repeated today over special schools.

Compulsory schooling began in 1870 although it was years until almost all children attended school. Disturbed or 'maladjusted' children and those with learning difficulties were always found by teachers to be a problem (Hurt, 1979; Cooter, 1992; Hendrick, 1997), and psychologists developed methods of testing and classifying them (Burt, 1925, 1937). Schools were largely funded through local authorities. This partly explains the lack of national standards and the great differences between LEAs in their policies, for example, about special schools. Some blind and deaf and 'delicate' pupils attended voluntary schools.

Only as recently as 1970, did an Education Act state that no child is 'ineducable' and that every child, however impaired, should attend school. Education authorities became responsible for every child, though the health services still share some duties. For example, some special schools are sited in hospitals, and statements of special educational need include medical reports. The steep rise in numbers of pupils with statements from 62,000 in January 1991 to 134,000 in January 1997 (DfEE, 1997a) partly reflects the parents' and teachers' anxieties about scarce resources, and the belief that extra help cannot be obtained without a statement.

By 1971, there were 1,019 special schools in England and Wales (Jowett, Hegarty, Moses, 1988) and 482 new ones opened during 1971–72 (DES, 1975). There are about the same number of special school places today (Norwich, 1994), about 98,000 places (DfEE, 1997a). Yet the 1981 Education Act gave LEAs the duty 'to secure that [a child with a statement of special education need] is educated in an ordinary school'. Today, pupils with physical, sensory and some learning difficulties are increasingly integrated into ordinary schools, and the literature about teaching them there is burgeoning (Lewis, 1991; Gross, 1993; Goddard and Tester, 1996; Cornwall, 1997). So why are almost two per cent of all pupils still taught in special schools and units? The question is considered through this book.

Topics and methods of the research

We asked for pupils' views and experiences about 'what kind of school is best for me?' How does a segregated or integrated placement affect my view of the world and of other people, and of who I am and want to be? Through observing and talking with them, we saw how young people's and adults' detailed experiences and reasoning, values and feelings influence their views about integration. Our study of special education is unusual in these respects:

in aiming to work from the perspectives of pupils and parents, at home and at school;

in considering their aspirations, as well as their current views and their memories, in order to see how pupils consider that schools further their present and future interests;

in combining interviews with observations to increase communication with young people with speech, learning and other difficulties who are rarely involved in research;

in relating the families and schools to their strongly contrasting LEAs' policies;

in describing inclusive and excluding policies, good and poor practices;

in analysing underlying reasons to show how and why good practice can be achieved.

We gave out printed and Braille copies of a short leaflet '*What kind of school is best for me?*' written for readers aged from about eight years or for parents to read to their children. It explained about the researchers, the research aims and questions, and the rights of people we hoped to interview. We also explained our work during our visits to schools and home interviews. Here is part of the leaflet:

> More disabled young people go to mainstream schools now, than they did a few years ago. Researchers have asked teachers, and other people working in education, about their views of these changes.
>
> But what do young people at school, and their parents, think about the changes? What impact have the changes made on their lives, and on their hopes for the future?
>
> Integrated education involves bringing disabled young people into mainstream schools. It can also mean everyone in the school getting on well together, and feeling an important member of their school. What kinds of schools, and teaching, can help young people to feel this way?
>
> Many disabled adults want the right to play a full part in society. What kinds of skills and rights do young people think that they need? How can schools best help them to gain these?

During semi–structured interviews we asked about daily life at school— lessons and other activities, friends, teachers, transport, discipline, assessments and statements of special educational need, help with any extra problems, moving between schools, why these moves were made and who decided about them—and about young people's views on their present and future interests. Everyone who was asked agreed to be tape–recorded and the recordings were transcribed. A few interviews lasted ten to fifteen minutes, many lasted over an hour or two. Most students were interviewed twice, one year apart, and the second interview followed up any changes during the year including changes of school.

We assured interviewees that 'there are no right or wrong answers, it is your views that matter'. We respected their views on the choice of topics and pace of the interview. Sometimes people seemed to us to ramble, but on rereading the scripts we saw useful new insights in these sections. When observing in classrooms, we acted as informal helpers if asked to do so. We sat at their tables with the students and aimed to set up informal friendly relations with them. Combining observations, and sometimes play sessions, with interviews and informal conversations helped us to communicate expressively with pupils who had little or no speech. We used the interpretive approaches other researchers have used (Oswin, 1971). We were welcomed by most students, including those labelled as having autism and severe communication disorders. School staff were also very helpful, though a few were unwilling to talk. After each school visit, we made detailed records, to use with the interview transcripts when writing reports. (For further discussion about methods, access and ethics in this study see Alderson and Goodey, 1996, and in special education generally see Clough and Barton, 1995.)

How general are our findings?

We are concerned to show the very wide range and variety of experiences, the importance of understanding people's views in the light of their own experiences and social context, their explanations and circumstances. We did not attempt to obtain a typical or representative sample, and are cautious about generalising from these examples. However, we involved young people with a wide range of difficulties and backgrounds. The two LEAs represent such opposite extremes along the spectrum from inclusive to segregated schooling that all other LEAs are likely to be similar or to fall between these extremes. The special EBD, MLD and SLD schools we visited are similar in some respects and are probably typical rather than exceptional. The teachers meet on courses and have often worked in several special schools, suggesting some homogeneity between schools. Where it is reasonable to generalise from our examples, we do so in these ways:

by relating our examples to the current context of English education, and to other research and reviews;

by showing how individual examples are influenced by general policies and practices, and general structures in schools;

by testing general assumptions, finding exceptions to them, and showing with our examples how some influential beliefs are misleading or unhelpful.

Despite the variety of individuals, difficulties and schools, strong themes repeatedly appeared. To avoid repetition in every chapter, and to assist readers in tracing the repeated themes, we consider the main ones here.

Effectiveness, good and poor practice

We will refer through the book to effective, good or poor practice. Despite the important and extensive literature on school effectiveness (Cooper 1993; Sammons *et al.*, 1995; Stoll and Fink, 1996) we found it hard to define detailed effectiveness. Deciding whether a school is effective involves deciding what schools are for and priorities differ. Schools are for: academic learning, to gain knowledge, critical understanding and qualifications; for vocational learning to qualify for future employment or further training; social learning, to live well with other people in small and large groups, to relate with care and respect, to have the confidence to tackle problems in positive ways, to become more aware of one's self and others, of moral and political values, and responsible citizenship and parenthood; cultural and creative learning, to transfer knowledge and attitudes to new generations, to help them to develop their skills and express themselves creatively; child care, in modern societies which assume that adults should guard children from dangers, idleness and vice (Qvortrup *et al.*, 1994) and that children with physical or behavioural difficulties need extra care or control; some special schools are mainly concerned with bodily and sensory care of impaired pupils, or managing the behaviour of disturbed ones.

The difficulty of assessing effectiveness in schools where learning is not the main concern is shown by OFSTED reports on special schools. These typically begin:

> The characteristics of the pupils for whom the school caters make it inappropriate to judge their attainment against age–related national expectations or averages. The report does give examples of what pupils know, understand and can do. Judgements about progress take account of information contained in pupils' Statements of Special Educational Need and annual reviews.

Yet statements and reviews are not simply factual, but are highly subjective and complicated (Galloway *et al.*, 1994). They may exaggerate difficulty in order to gain resources. West County SEN audit forms ask for a single tick on global complex topics like a pupil's 'confidence in executing task' or 'outwardness and sociability'. OFSTED uses such loose measures to support general unexplained conclusions: an EBD boarding school where places cost £35,000 each per year is described as having low standards but 'reasonable costs'. Nearby mainstream primary places cost about £1,400 per year, and secondary places cost about £2,500; West County special school day places usually cost from £7,000–£14,000 each.

We interpreted effectiveness in several ways. How did schools help students to learn in academic, social and cultural ways? Were they, for example, taught things they already knew, or possibly being misinformed? From many observed examples: an EBD school lesson on the difference between boats and ships, which claimed that ships, unlike boats, have bedrooms and transport food, did not count as effective teaching. At the end of the lesson, four girls sang to the class. Three giggled their way through nursery rhythms, but when the fourth dreamily sang 'Bright eyes', everyone listened intently then clapped enthusiastically, so that the moments seemed 'effective' for social and cultural learning. The OFSTED report of this school commended a lesson about cells in the human body, during which students drew a body shape on graph paper and coloured in the squares to help them to understand cells. To imply that cells are like a patchwork costume we count as misleading rather than informative teaching. At the visual impairment school, students were helped to produce and debate reasons for and against new towns in ways that seemed 'effectively' to expand their knowledge, critical understanding, and confidence in arguing their case.

We also considered how much time was spent on learning and interactions, or on passive waiting. How positive did the interactions and teachers' comments about pupils seem? When there were problems, were pupils treated as the problem or involved as part of the solution? How fair did the rewards and punishments seem to be? We report our observations, and the teachers' and students' comments. Effectiveness can be examined through these processes, and also through outcomes, which include external test and examination results, though special schools which opt out of these lack clear outcome measures.

Defining and assessing difficulties

Some experts assume that defining and assessing impairments and disturbance is clear–cut (Hoghughi *et al.*, 1992), others disagree (Gould, 1984; Briggs and Statham, 1985). In practice, definitions can be complicated and elusive.

Learning difficulties

Children with severe learning difficulties may be quick–witted and humorous, the most profoundly affected children can have intense feelings and awareness about relationships (Oswin, 1971). Everyone has learning difficulties, from young children learning to read to academics poring over learned texts, and teachers generally are mainly concerned with helping their students to overcome such difficulties. This raises questions about whether moderate or severe learning difficulties are qualitatively different, and actually need different teaching techniques, from ordinary learning difficulties. Learning difficulties are affected by their context, such as the type of teaching, so that assessments need to take account of this, as well as of how the assessors' own methods, values and relationship with the student might affect the assessment. The weakness in the Warnock Report is often pointed out, in that it treats a mutable and even arbitrarily evolved context and provision almost as if it is static and absolute, when saying that:

> there should be a system of recording as in need of special educational provision those children who, on the basis of a detailed profile of their needs prepared by a multi–disciplinary team, are judged by their local education authority to require special provision not generally available in ordinary schools (DES, 1987:3.31).

Students may have learning difficulties with one teacher, method or assessor, but not with others. Perceptions of severe learning difficulties differ. Tracey (in chapter 4) is seen as different at her comprehensive school although not by her parents and neighbours. George (in chapter 4), who spoke eloquently for two hours covering a wide range of personal and political topics, attends an SLD school. Standardised assessments take little account of context so, for example, George's parents' knowledge of his abilities contradict the psychologist's brief assessment, leaving the 'real' level of his difficulty uncertain.

Emotional and behavioural difficulties
Criteria for defining and assessing EBD are still more uncertain. EBD is often implicitly discussed as if it is an illness, a fact like cancer, which needs expert treatment, but it can be vague and variable. A single response might be condemned by one person, excused by another, or seen as reasonable, or prevented by other observers. EBD is constructed in how observers variously perceive it, and also in how it is prompted or shaped by circumstances. Katie (in chapter 2) shows how girls at her EBD school are stuck into negative reactions. Philip's father attributes Philip's disturbance partly to angry teachers; 'healing' comes when Philip and the teachers learn to behave differently. When EBD is seen as attention deficit hyperactivity disorder, the medical model becomes so dominant that Ritalin is increasingly prescribed (Levy, 1997; Maras *et al.*, 1997; Wright, 1997). Yet the ensuing problems of the medical approach include: risks of exaggerating the disturbance; diagnoses that may become self–fulfilling prophesies; assumptions that disturbance is only in the child

and not also in the context, and that expert adults are required to cure the problem; and incentives for adults to exaggerate and perpetuate problems, to gain higher attendance benefits for the family or allowances for the school.

Uncertainty on the individual level is repeated at the general level. Have students become much more badly behaved in recent years, as many teachers claim? An apparently great increase in disturbance is indicated by rates of permanent exclusions, from about 3,000 in 1990 to over 11,000 in 1993/4 and 1994/5, and 13,500 in 1995/6 with many thousands more informal exclusions (Schools Minister's report to the National Children's Bureau conference, reported in *The Guardian*, 10.7.96, p 10; it is hard to obtain formal figures). This increase has coincided with great increases in poverty and deprivation for children in the UK (Lansdown and Newell, 1994; Wilkinson, 1994). One in three children now grows up in poverty and many others live on the edges of poverty. There is increasing physical restriction of children and adult control over their time and space (Qvortrup *et al.*, 1994). Playgrounds, parks and fields where they once played energetically are now largely deserted for fear of strangers and dangers. The Education Reform Act (DES, 1988) introduced the national curriculum with added administrative duties for teachers, and greater pressures on staff and students to work academically and competitively; these can add to the difficulties for non–academic pupils. Competition between schools, the league tables, the need to attract parents to enrol their children and thus to assure the school income, growing cost consciousness at every level of management, and less funding for competing 'extras', such as special needs resources, have led to growing regimentation in schools; as factories abandon impersonal conveyor belt methods, schools increasingly enforce them (Jeffs, 1995). Teachers' fears about their school gaining a poor reputation and 'being named and shamed' further discourage them from being flexible and giving their scarce time to disturbed students.

Autistic spectrum disorder (ASD)
Autism is generally assumed to be an extreme form of emotional disturbance (Wing, 1981; Frith, 1989), a physiological and perhaps genetic disorder. Diagnosis of ASD brings several benefits. Parents and teachers can feel relieved that they are not to blame for a condition which is medical. They can feel that the more severe the child's condition, the more compassionate, rather than futile or even harmful, their efforts have been. They need not feel 'bad' if they cannot affect a seemingly intractable problem. Children benefit when they are no longer regarded as naughty or lazy or wilfully refusing to improve, and they can be understood with greater sympathy and tolerance. They are more likely to gain access to extra and special resources.

However, there are disadvantages in diagnosing ASD. Attributing cause to a fault of whatever kind in the child links blame to the child in many complex ways. Adults may examine their own responses less critically, and dismiss the child's rational protests, distress or anger simply as evidence of ASD. All difficulty may be assumed to rest in the child and all the goodness in the adults. There is a danger of seeing the child as irrational and listening less carefully, which is likely to increase the child's frustration and misbehaviour. Assuming a medical cause does not necessarily make irritating symptoms any less irritating, or invest adults with more patience; they may have less hope and faith in their work, and reinterpret ordinary behaviour in pathological terms. The problem of distinguishing between deliberate or involuntary misbehaviour remains, with dilemmas about using positive or negative discipline. Adults' expectations may be so low that the child's abilities pass unrecognised, valuable opportunities are lost, and low expectations become self–fulfilling. As with all other difficulties, adults may feel they need to exaggerate severity to gain more resources or support. Deterioration may be accepted not as evidence of teachers' failure, but as their success or heroism, in 'proving' that they contend with such serious problems.

However, as illustrated in chapter 3, ASD combines many characteristics, and none are necessary or sufficient for a diagnosis of such a vague collection of disorders. All but two of the eighteen children in the autistic unit we observed clearly showed 'normal', non–autistic competencies, so the point to their being there was unclear.

Physical and sensory impairments
Impairments of the body would seem to be far easier to define and assess precisely than problems of the mind. Inability to see or walk is a medical–scientific fact requiring special teaching aids, even if emotional or learning difficulties are not. Yet the degree of impairment does not necessarily relate to how disabled these pupils are by circumstances. Having to rely on a wheelchair is not a problem in accessible schools and buses (Oliver, 1996), and a blind man can be Secretary of State for Education and Employment. Chapter 5 shows how schools for physical and sensory impairments do not simply accept the most severely disabled students.

Selecting students

Some schools are defined as special because they admit a specially selected group of students with particular special needs. But when the original difficulty or impairment is hard to assess precisely, then it is uncertain whom the schools should admit, and why. Further complications arise when many special school staff feel that they now have less control over the selection of their pupils and that their schools are being filled by LEAs with more disturbed and excluded pupils. The head of a small unit originally for convalescent teenagers said that it was being changed by the LEA into a pupil referral unit for excluded teenagers and also for young people having psychiatric treatment. 'We've been sent five young people who attempted suicide last term, but we have no psychological support at all.'

Can EBD schools be defined by their students, in that they are all obviously more disturbed than students in mainstream schools? Our study confirms other research findings on the difficulties of selecting the most disturbed students (Potts and Statham, 1985; Briggs, 1985). Research which compared records of boys admitted to a secure unit with those of boys who were refused admission found no obvious differences between the two sets (Kelly, 1992). After minor offences, some boys were admitted without any of the formal admission procedures which had excluded boys with much more serious records. Education and social service referral records of disturbed behaviour are arbitrary in several ways, influenced as we have mentioned by the attitudes of the record keepers, and their relationship with the student being assessed. Boys, those with moderate learning difficulties, and especially African Caribbean boys are greatly over–represented in special schools (Lansdown and Newell, 1994), and in being treated as SEN in mainstream schools (Daniels *et al.*, 1997). We met boys and girls managing well in mainstream school, who had far more serious communication difficulties than many pupils in EBD or SLD schools. In East City's mainstream classes it was self–evident why pupils were there; either it was their local school or, in a few cases such as the deaf students or those with profound and multiple learning difficulties, the school had been resourced with British sign language signers or other extra support. Yet many pupils in the EBD schools we observed behaved politely and responsibly. Did this mean they were disturbed all the time, or that they had occasional outbursts? If so, how frequent or severe must the outbursts be before someone qualifies as EBD? The staff sometimes mentioned adverse home circumstances as grounds for referral for some pupils, rather than educational need, as if the parents were EBD rather than the child.

Remit, aims and methods

Apart from the complications in assessment and selection, there is still the question: if pupils have difficulties with feeling, talking, behaving or relating, why put them into a school or class where all the members have similar or more severe difficulties? If 'milder' cases adopt the more unusual sounds and gestures made by other pupils, how much of this is due to imitation, or to resorting to behaviours which are clearly rewarded with the teachers' attention (as in the special schools we observed)? At the SLD school, unusual noises and table manners were very obvious at lunch time. In contrast, at the crowded dining halls at East City schools, pupils with severe learning and behaviour difficulties mixed unobtrusively with their peers who gave ample examples of ordinary, polite behaviour.

It is also hard to see precisely how pupils' education in, say, reading, maths, history or art is different because they cannot walk or speak and have a physical or psychological problem. What special or unique expertise do EBD teachers have? What are their appropriate teaching methods that differ from competent mainstream teachers' approaches to learning and behavioural difficulties? (McNamara and Moreton, 1993, 1995, 1997; Rudduck, 1996). The special schools we observed did not, on the whole, offer a superior academic or social education. Yet paradoxically, the more vague a professional skill is, the more mystified, impressed and inadequate 'lay' people can feel, including parents and mainstream teachers (Tomlinson, 1982; Galloway, 1994).

The most purposeful special school we saw was Louis Braille. Even here, when blind students have the necessary extra equipment, expert teaching largely involves methods and relationships which would benefit any group of students, such as empathising with the student and helping with any difficulties. Key differences with visual impairment include teaching Braille and mobility skills to those who need them, relying much more on touch and sound, and devising tactile aids and ways of explaining mainly visual concepts. Yet boarding students at Louis Braille who go daily into ordinary schools and colleges show that these supports can be used in a range of settings. Parents are the main teachers during the first three most crucial learning years and skilled preventative help when at home could perhaps help to reduce the need for special centres later. Uncertainty about a school's remit and methods leads on to more general problems. When special schools are uncertain, it is not clear how they are better for any students than an effective mainstream school would be. Vague aims are associated with a vague curriculum and uncertain, circular daily activities, with loss of a sense of purpose for the staff. It is then harder for the students to know how to co-operate with them. Instead of being remedial and reintegration centres, special EBD and MLD schools' role is mainly non-educational, to contain, and if they make little difference to students' problems the reasons for referral are unclear. Special schooling isolates pupils as different and inferior with lasting personal and social consequences which may be blamed on the original difficulty. Emotional and learning difficulties are linked through cause and effect, like frustration and boredom, failure and anger. Undue emphasis on medical or psychological causes can stop teachers from thinking creatively about educational issues. Narrow repetitiveness when assumed to be a symptom of autism can be used to excuse lack of well–prepared and varied teaching.

As we have shown, West County is a highly segregated area with many specialist schools selecting for ability, income and social background, religion, sex and behaviour. This would seem to be a logically planned system to ensure that a suitable school is provided for each individual. Yet it creates a paradox. The more highly specialised and selective each school is, the more intolerant and excluding it can also become. Instead of schools being designed to fit pupils, pupils are expected to fit the school. The narrower the remit of the school, the harder it can be for the students to fit the required type, and the wider the gaps between schools through which students can fall into exclusion.

When in the education 'market' pupils become the commodities, and also the 'window dressing' to attract new customers, disturbed young people are not wanted. Teachers feel under greater pressure to insist on compliance; it is harder for them to tolerate and take time to address problems of behaviour and learning. Large scale intolerance of difficulties leading to thousands of exclusions penetrates to the smallest daily details of teachers' decisions, whether to exclude or accommodate, to punish or work on promoting positive behaviour. These decisions are influenced by the time, resources and support which teachers have to help them to attend to behaviour problems. The limitations in official advice on EBD to teachers, such as in DES (1989) which emphasises superficial and punitive control rather than help with resolving causes of poor behaviour, have been publicised (Cooper and Upton, 1990). Competitive systems which allow less or even 'zero' tolerance are liable to increase disturbed pupils' anxiety, loneliness and sense of rejection and exacerbate their antisocial behaviour. Complaints from other students and their parents increase pressure on teachers to try to enforce control through punishment or exclusion which is increasingly accepted as an inevitable and appropriate measure. The effect in West County is rising exclusion rates and students who spend many months at home waiting to be accepted by another school.

In contrast, exclusion numbers have fallen in East City over the past three years, though the borough has no EBD schools and the national trend is rising. The head of behaviour support services in East City sees efforts to integrate statemented students and to reduce exclusion rates as connected, each is useless without the other. 'A policy of inclusion for statemented pupils can't work where there is a culture of exclusion,' and efforts to avoid exclusion work as 'background radiation' for successfully including statemented pupils. About 80 per cent of statemented EBD pupils remain for five years at their mainstream secondary school in East City. More are expected to do so as schools build on 'the present foundations of the wider culture of inclusion'.

Auditing schools

West County has an elaborate schools funding system based, not on social measures like the number of pupils having free school meals, but on reported need. Teachers score students on a scale from 1–6 and submit reports and examples of pupil's work. Teacher moderators only check sample schools, and it is hard to see how, for instance, emotional difficulties can be assessed without seeing the student or the school. Although the manual states that the context should be taken into account, the recording methods largely prevent this. The schema also individualises problems back into each pupil, shifting attention away from socio–economic or whole school factors, although the funds are explicitly granted to the whole school and not individual pupils.

Conflict between financial and educational values was shown when a teacher spoke of having a 'bad year' when the special school budget fell because the students' difficulties were assessed as less severe: educational gain but financial loss. There are strong, hidden disincentives for special school staff. If they help students to improve and return to mainstream, the special school income and rolls will fall, staff have to leave, other teachers are absent while they support reintegration, the remaining staff have more work, and the school may become unviable.

In mainstream schools, the greater the students' reported failures and difficulties. the more the calibre of the staff is questioned. Yet in special schools, the greater the reported difficulties, the more competent and even heroic the staff can appear to be, in dealing with such serious, intractable cases. If many special school ex–students end up in a mental hospital, prison or other institution (and far too little is known about the longer–term outcomes of special schools) this too can be taken as evidence to show the immense difficulties the school staff contend with, rather than to question their competence. Similarly, on an individual level, special school students' protests, boredom and unhappiness tend to be interpreted as evidence of their own difficulty and disturbance and not as serious commentaries on their teaching. Severe unhappiness and disturbance in day special schools are even taken to indicate the need for a boarding place.

An indication that these are national problems, and are not confined to the schools we observed, is the extremely low return rate of students from special schools back into mainstream ones (Audit Commission, 1992). This suggests that some schools may simply be 'dumping grounds' (Norwich, 1996:36) for pupils no one knows what to do with. As we discuss later, most special educational 'treatments' are either controversial (Christensen and Fazal, 1996; Hornby *et al.*, 1997) or consist of good recommended teaching methods that mainly apply to all pupils, leaving the extra help which special schools can offer unclear.

EBD schools face dilemmas shared by prisons. Should they emphasise reform, punishment, or retribution on wrong–doers? As prisons change their emphases, punitive or reformative, over the decades, it is likely that EBD schools reflect them and changing public opinion. Policies are influenced by historical and religious beliefs about 'can or will', about whether disturbed young people cannot help behaving badly (they are sick or mad and to be pitied) or could will themselves to behave better (they are bad and must be corrected or punished). Staff in EBD schools we observed tend to veer between being pitying and punitive, sympathetic and seeming to provoke students as if to test whether they are improving or to create opportunities to teach self–control.

As in adult society, some students are at times too ill or too dangerous to be able to attend school. Some have severe mental illness and need psychiatric treatment. But the great majority in special schools are not ill, and if they are, special schools cannot provide appropriate medical help.

Parents' choice

To provide a range of special schools is supposed to offer parents 'a continuum of choice', as if choice has to mean sites and not services. Yet special schools can limit choice. Pupils' personalities and needs cannot be confined to the narrow label EBD or SLD. The schools in West County show how a fixed range of special schools leads to supply–led services and not choice–led service. LEAs need to keep certain expensive special school places filled. Pupils with multiple difficulties may not fit anywhere. Stacey was thought to be too bright for her SLD school and too impaired for the school for physically impaired students. Nicholas was excluded from his EBD school for being disruptive. Hundreds of West County children also go to 'out–of–borough' special schools, often boarding ones. By law, their parents can be refused a mainstream place (Spendiff v North Tyneside Council, 1997; Crane v Lancashire County Council, 1997) though this is a right of all parents of 'normal' children. The choice tends to be for the schools to select and reject students and thus limit families' choices.

One choice for parents is between small special schools or units on the same site as mainstream schools. These are often referred to as 'integrated', and sessions with other schools may be listed in notices. We found that very little if any integration occurs between the same–site schools observed; they may be as remote from one another as if they were miles apart, and parents may be unaware of the isolation.

The opposite approach in East City is to have wide–remit inclusive schools which adapt to the students. Philip and Ben show (in chapters 2 and 4) how this accepting cooperation can reduce and prevent difficulties, and enable students to become better at adapting to the school. A much richer and more flexible range of choices, of staff, services, other students and resources, can be offered in larger ordinary schools than in the relatively small special schools. Real choices are informed ones, and one purpose of this book is to inform the wider general public about special and ordinary school options to help them to make informed choices.

Links with home

Special schools are recommended as able to give more personal care in closer contact with parents (for example, DES, 1989). Yet it is often much harder for parents to keep in contact with a distant unit. One head teacher said, 'We say a one hour journey is the limit, but when several children are picked up in the rush hour it can be more than that'. There is little of the informal daily contact parents have with local primary school. When children have communication difficulties , it is harder for parents to discover what they did during the day, and more so when they have less contact with other children and parents at the school. Parents mentioned feeling daunted by the staff, and ignorant about their children's needs for expertise; some added that they felt the staff treated them as stupid or abnormal. When we approached parents through informal networks or through the schools for visual and physical impairments we had high response rates. When we sent letters through the SLD, MLD, EBD and autism schools none replied. Staff in these schools told us of parents' apparent unwillingness to contact the school, and added other possible reasons: it is harder to arrange child care for these pupils, so parents are less able to attend evening meetings; they may have less time and energy, for example, to serve as governors; in a small school it is harder to find candidates. 'It is always the same few who offer to help and we have far fewer of them.' Parents reported that some schools did not have regular home–school contact books, 'they were knocked on the head years ago', and homework was not regularly set by the special schools observed apart from Louise Braille school except, it appears, when an OFSTED inspection is due.

Small classes, one–to–one teaching

EBD students are assumed to need 'one–to–one' teaching, extra and individual attention and high staff–pupil ratios implying many extra hours of personal tuition, but these are not necessarily a bonus. They often involve either tuition for one child while the rest wait or 'play', or else one single task for the whole class, regardless of their varying abilities, with the teacher seeming unable or unwilling to offer more than one activity at once. Each child may do a task in turn with interruptions while the bored ones are disciplined, and the assistants chat, make tea, or simply watch.

Small classes can be as noisy and disruptive as large ones, as if some pupils fill whatever space and time is available; a few pupils can take up almost all the teachers' attention, whilst others endure, tolerate or condone the disruption. Small classes of pupils, all selected because of their 'special' difficulties and very diverse needs, can be harder to organise than large classes with a core of 'ordinary' and committed pupils. Teams of staff share groups of pupils when small classes are highly staffed, and when classes are combined to give staff non–contact time. 'Special' attention, in the sense of special continuing knowledge of a pupil or special rapport, is then less likely to be achieved. Yet continuity is thought to be vital for students with learning difficulties when subtle changes in numerous terms, such as saying 'times' or 'multiply', or even in the way a letter or number is written, can make all the difference between clarity and confusion (Lewis, 1995).

One–to–one methods are very useful in teaching but, when they are used almost exclusively, pupils can feel distant from one another. This is in contrast to the more warmly supportive classroom dynamics of schools which encourage positive peer involvement described at the end of chapter 2. Isolated pupils are more likely to feel suspicious and hostile and to feel mistrusted and disliked by others (Mosley, 1993; McNamara and Moreton, 1995). Over–use of one–to–one methods can implicitly denigrate pupils, by exaggerating their dependence on adults and implying that they have nothing positive to offer one another. They can get trapped into negative regress, and learned helplessness (Coopersmith, 1967; Seligman, 1975) reinforced by taught helplessness. They are prevented from sharing activities, experiences and mutual rewarding support and trust with friends at school, and often attendance at special school means they have no friends at home.

Some staff in EBD and MLD schools actively keep pupils apart, telling them not to help or to trust one another, not 'to interfere and make trouble between yourselves', to refer all questions or problems to the staff, and to report other pupils' misbehaviour. This can undermine the encouragement of self–confidence and responsibility for oneself and for others; these qualities are shown by students in schools that encourage positive peer interactions. If high staffing ratios discourage independence and interdependence, they reinforce assumptions that students are solely a cost and a liability, and are not themselves resources and contributors, who can assist the staff and one another. As the end of chapter 2 shows, seeing students as positive contributors opens the way to resolving EBD problems.

The order of the book

We begin with emotional and behavioural difficulty (EBD) because this is the most common reason for referral to special school, alone or combined with other difficulties. Chapter 2 compares the range of special schools in West County, with ordinary comprehensive schools in East City. How are the schools suited to the students, or the students expected to adapt to the schools? Which system is more flexible, efficient and humane? How are EBD students identified, and what is appropriate discipline for them? The chapter considers expectations and 'games' played in EBD schools, and the schools' remit and aims. The special teaching skills of EBD school staff are reviewed, and chapter 2 ends with examples of ordinary, or inclusive, schools which promote positive behaviour, and a summary of why their structures allow more innovative approaches than special schools are liable to risk taking.

Chapter 3 examines what is assumed to be the medical extreme of disturbance, autistic spectrum disorders. It examines meanings of autism and of the spectrum and compares experiences in an autistic unit in West County with two ordinary schools in East City. Chapter 4 on learning difficulties looks at the context, and compares students in West County SLD and MLD schools with those in East City comprehensive schools; Vishal has Down's syndrome, Tracey illustrates views on 'backwardness', and Ben has moderate learning difficulties. Chapter 5 describes special and inclusive schools in West County, and reports the views and experiences of physically and visually impaired students. The experiences of students with physical and hearing impairments in ordinary schools in East City are then reviewed.

Chapter 6 takes the framework of the Convention on the Rights of the Child (UN, 1989), which considers all children's interests under the headings of provision, protection and participation. It discusses what is special about special schools in terms of extra provision, resources, services and expertise, extra protections from stress, and the risk of failure and bullying, and how special and ordinary schools support young people's participation. How do they equip students socially and academically to enable them to participate in 'the real world' at home, school, their community and later at work and as adult citizens? Finally, we consider changes at every level to make inclusive education work (see table 1 above).

Chapter 2

EMOTIONAL AND BEHAVIOURAL DIFFICULTIES

Lucy: 'I think we should behave ourselves.
We should learn without needing this [behaviour management].'

Emotional and behavioural difficulty is very hard to define (House of Commons, 1997), as is 'normal behaviour'. Thousands of children and teenagers live in a borderland, perceived by some adults as disturbed and by others as normal. They contribute positively to one group and disrupt another. As the following chapters show, uncertainties in defining and assessing emotional and behavioural difficulites (EBD) lead on to confusion about how to treat it or to assess the effects of treatment. Nicholas was moved from school to school in West County. His experience raises questions about the logic of providing a wide range of different specialist schools. How does that system compare with one that has a few broadly similar types of wide–ability mainstream schools which Philip experienced? Which system is the more flexible, efficient and humane? Lucy's and Katie's special schooling and Sean's mainstream schooling illustrate the impact of people's expectations about behaviour on actual behaviour. They also show the importance of adults being aware of their own behaviour and of psychological games and exploitation, if they are to help disturbed children and teenagers. Terry's experience of special school continues the theme of how schools appear to allow, constrain or compel certain reactions in their students and staff, sometimes unintentionally, so raising the questions: What is special about EBD schools? What is the actual nature of emotions and behaviour, and how they can be changed? Unless school staff discuss their views and reach some agreement, their conflicting views could be said to sabotage their best efforts. The final section reports innovative ways of promoting positive behaviour in schools and considers the use of these methods in mainstream and special schools.

To fit the students to the school or the school to the students?

Nicholas in West County

Nicholas lives near a boys' secondary modern school with 'special needs' streams, but attended an EBD school known locally as one 'for difficult kids' eighteen miles away. He had begun to stay in respite care one week in three.

He lives in a small flat with his father on a council estate, where the edge of the village meets the fields. Both his parents had attended schools for learning difficulties. Nicholas was eleven at the time of his first interview at home, quiet and shy at first, half watching television, he gradually became more interested in the interview.

His father, Jack, described the 'father and son' activities they enjoy together: camping with friends, and photographing wild life. Nicholas then brought out photos of himself doing these activities, leading a friend's heavy horses to display their winning rosettes, and mucking out their stables. He is not afraid of the huge beasts 'though they nip you with their teeth, ow!' He hopes to work with them when he leaves school. He fetched his school books to show his maths, writing and his project on the Victorians. He jumped around excitedly, and hugged the interviewer and offered 'any tea or coffee darling?'. 'He misses his mother', said his father, showing photos of them camping. Nicholas showed his big collection of camping stickers.

Interviewer: How many camps have you been to?

Nicholas: Hundreds, darling.

Jack: At the last count we had fifty–six, we've added two more since then. There's the cathedral where I was on duty for St. John's ambulance. The Archbishop and the Pope walked past me and I could have virtually touched them.

Nicholas: And me, and me. I got posters, and a postcard of that. Look, look, cathedral.

Jack: Yes, we climbed up to the top.

Nicholas: Stained glass, look in my book, in that green book, I like that.

Jack: Yes, and we belong to the ramblers association, he's a good walker, he'll do twelve miles no problems at all, be the fittest one of the lot.

Nicholas said that he cooked 'spagtibolnais—spa–ghetti bolog–naise' at school 'and dough to make a pizza'. At home, he looks at their videos and fine books on natural history, while Jack is at work. Occasionally he plays football with two other boys in the road lined with parked cars. Jack said, 'every other word a swear word, you know, and one is a coloured neighbour' (in an area where almost everyone is white).

Jack's constant hope is that Nicholas will 'go into mainstream', but at the annual reviews 'each year they recommend another year up there (special school) 'cos he's definitely improving and I think, fair enough they're the experts, hopefully they'll get it right'. Yet a year later, Nicholas was at an SLD school, after months at home excluded from school, because he 'went berserk in the classroom' at the EBD school. From being slim and lively, he had become overweight, with a dull expression; his school shirt was stained with food, like those of other pupils at the SLD school. Other schools refused to accept him. The SLD school teachers were very concerned at the disruption Nicholas created among their mainly passive pupils and wanted to move him to an MLD school in another area. The long taxi journeys and the level of learning in the SLD school did not help him to be calmer in class.

Philip in East City

When he was seven Philip's mother left home and the two boys were going to be put into care. His father, Andy, gave up work in order to look after his sons, they became homeless and lived in bed and breakfast for a while. Philip had bowel problems and his father remembered, 'he was in and out of hospital for tests but it didn't get any better'. Philip would 'go for little walks' as his father said, and be brought back by the police. He was in trouble at school for 'throwing books, pushing chairs over, screaming and things like that'. Andy saw rationality in Philip's behaviour at the infant school.

> He could only concentrate on something for about five minutes, then he'd want to go and do something else. He couldn't sit and listen to a story, it was too boring for him... He wanted to do something else... and because he wasn't getting it he was losing his temper, ranting and raving... If someone was having a go at him, he just shut down in a little world of his own. I didn't know anything was wrong.

Philip spent five months out of school waiting for a statement of special educational need, then he went to an EBD school. It was due to close and only five pupils remained there. Philip began to attend a mainstream primary school part time. Andy said,

> He was concentrating on what he was doing, he was helping everybody else in the class, he was actually instructing the other children in the class what to do with their work, and they said that's good. He was beginning to cope with stress. If they were having a barney, Philip would sit there nice and calmly. Then he also can control his temper. So if he was really angry he wouldn't take it out on other people. He wouldn't shout and scream or make a riot, he'd go for a little walk out of the classroom. Two minutes later comes back in, sits down nice and calm, just as if it hadn't happened. But they did say like, if people had a go at him it increased his anger. So now he's at secondary school, full–time and with no extra support.

The interviewer asked Philip about his SATs. Andy didn't know what these were but Philip showed his SATs work saying in a pleased tone, 'English I got 3, science I got 4, maths I got 3.' He takes the twenty–minute walk to school and likes exploring the city using his travel card, and no longer needs to attend the hospital. He enjoys writing and making up games. 'He'd rather be the team leader telling everybody what to do, organising, that's what he's good at, putting rules down. He doesn't like it if somebody disagrees with his rules.'

Philip is doing well at the secondary school, though he thinks the teaching is rather boring and strict. In an aggressive tone he says, 'Just get on with your work. Just put down what's on the board and GET ON WITH YOUR WORK!' He enjoys dinner time most and 'talking with me mates.'

At a play scheme, his father thinks Philip became bored and angry, and felt 'picked on'.

> He'd go off for a little walk, he liked to have his own space, calm down then he'd come back. They didn't know this so they'd go hounding him, shout and bawl at him, telling him off, things like that, giving him real bad grief, and it winds him up more. And he'd swear back at them and lose his temper, really bad, and then they'd have a go at me: 'Philip's been abusive.' But Philip's not like that. [I said to the staff] 'You're not trained at all, you don't know what you're doing.'

Philip's father thinks that his worst time was before Philip was excluded from primary school. Teachers were:

> shouting and bawling at him, screaming at him, which at the time it would make him worse. As soon as they were out of distance he would feel all right again. Nobody knew what was going on in his head... there was no one helping him—it was just, oh blame all of it on Philip. It would spark him off, he would just rant and rave and scream, shout, which used to make me mad; I used to think there should be someone here to help us.
>
> [The best moment was] getting him into [comprehensive] secondary school with no problems like what he'd been through. He's settled in, he's just like any normal kid, without anything wrong with him and any problems... With Philip, I talk to him like an adult now, I mean I always have. To me, he's just another adult but with a younger brain. Because they are people... Even though his brother's eight, he's still a person. Now if you treat them like an idiot, they'll look at you like an idiot.

When talking about the family budget or planning weekends or attending a funeral, 'they understood and we all talked about it like adults'.

Nicholas and Philip illustrate the common finding that when people feel respected (being treated as reasonable and reliable) and trusted (such as when working with the heavy horses) they show that they can be mature and reliable. They also illustrate a general point, affecting many other students: that inclusive schools which are willing to adapt to a range of types of student can reduce and prevent problems which less tolerant schools with a narrower remit can increase.

'Special children', discipline and justice

Lucy in West County

Lucy like Nicholas lives on a council estate on the edge of a village. Socially and academically, they are secluded at the margin of affluent neighbourhoods. The beautiful views initially distract the observer from the realities of social isolation, infrequent public transport and small, expensive, local shops. Blinds are closed on all the windows in Lucy's house because her parents, Ann and John, dislike the neighbours looking in. Lucy's daily forty miles on the school bus would involve four trains and four buses by public transport. When she was five, Lucy was referred to an MLD school for deaf children. When she was seven, her younger step brother went into care and she started boarding at that school. Ann said that Lucy had 'set her heart on going to a midstream school (sic), she calls that a proper school'. When aged twelve, Lucy was referred to an MLD/EBD school for language difficulties, and at fourteen to an EBD school. She was interviewed when aged thirteen, and the day after her fifteenth birthday when the living room was decorated with two large Christmas cards from her mother and stepfather to each other but with no other Christmas or birthday cards. Some of her statements record that she has good hearing and 'normal ability', though her parents repeatedly emphasise her limitations.

Ann: She's had operations since she was three years old, grommets five
        or six times, adenoids out twice [sic] then they done a brain scan on
        her this year, and they're telling me she's not deaf and she never has
        been, it's more/
John: /her brain/
Ann: /her brain, it's not functioning ... she got to this stage where if she
        didn't understand she'd say 'pardon?' and people would think there
        was something wrong in there ... She's got a good long term memory,
        but she hasn't got a short term memory. If I ask her 'What did you
        have for lunch at school?' she can't remember.

Lucy: I can't remember what I have for lunch.
Ann: And I have to watch her all the time, or she'd just wander off and get lost, she wouldn't understand.
Lucy: I'd just wander off.
Ann: So I can't ever let her out of my sight.
John: She's not getting any activities like other children. All she's got is her bedroom. She'd rather be out with the other girls.
Ann: She wants to be out and she can't understand why I won't let her. I can't trust her, even the head teacher told me there is no way I can let Lucy out to play... Lucy's taken to lying and the lying's getting worse.
John: Like at school she says she gets picked on ...
Ann: She said the teachers wouldn't let her go to the toilet and she started wetting. We had that for nine months. I think she doesn't like it at that school...
John: It used to be a borstal school for bad boys, then it changed to children with bad habits. ...
Ann: And Lucy's got in with them and now she's being like them.

Lucy appeared to enjoy her long interviews and confirmed her father's earlier account.

Lucy: I like computers. We've got a Nimbus, yes it's quite good.
Int: Do the teachers know how to use them?
Lucy: [shakes her head] All they know is they've got a computer in their office. Mr. Green knows how to use that, but the Nimbus, even, like the boys they don't know how to put them in.
Int: They have to call you to do it? [Lucy nods] And you know how to? [She nods.] Where did you learn?
Lucy: At me other school, we had a Nimbus at me other school.

While in her bedroom, Lucy was playing tunes on her keyboard by ear, and teaching herself to type, but her parents continued to emphasise her failings and her assessment, when aged eleven, of having a 'mental age of seven'.

Ann: She wanders off. She wouldn't be able to catch a bus home, plus she's too familiar with adults and she would go off. She's easily tempted, my daughter. It doesn't matter how much you drum it in. Like crossing the road, even at school, they have to grab her or she's gone, things, you know, that a seven–year–old would...
John: She's picked up every day by bus for school.

Int: And does she mind that?
Ann: Er ye–es and no. I don't really know. I don't think she wants to
        upset the house. I have terrible trouble getting her to tell me what's
        wrong... But she knows it's the only way and the only place she can go
        to.
John: She doesn't like the school.
Int: Might you have tried an ordinary school?
Ann: She's too backward.

Lucy's parents emphasised her need for constant attendance, and that the
school did not guard her carefully enough, as she had once ran away and
found her way home, a remarkable feat for someone who always travelled by
car or the school bus. Lucy's parents complained that her attendance allowance
had been reduced. They had 'battled' to have the allowance increased again
and kept saying it was essential to watch Lucy constantly. Her mother criticised
Lucy's teachers, but also sympathised with them.

Ann: She was a lovely child.. Her key worker is not satisfied that she's in
        the right school because her behavioural problems have got worse. I
        mean I love her but sometimes I really don't like her, 'cos you just
        can't talk to her. She's so moody all the time.
John: Making signs behind your back and/
Ann: /I know—a thirteen–year–old, being a teenager, they probably all
        do it—but it's even worse being her, and if it's because she's really
        unhappy... I think it sort of came out that she thought we'd put her in
        there [junior boarding school] just to get rid of her. But there was nothing
        else we could do ... But there's always one bad apple, and Lucy's got
        in with them and now she's being like them. She had a behavioural
        problem but now she's got a nasty behavioural problem. She was the
        only girl in the class and she's been stabbed, had bricks thrown at her,
        she's had/
John: /scissors in her eye nearly/
Ann: /her coat put down the toilet/
John: /still can't get the money for that, we're fighting that/
Ann: /and I think she's getting worse and worse... [explains how she
        thought the problem was mainly with the teachers, and then how she
        happened to visit the school] And Lucy didn't see me, I was standing
        in a corner, and she [Lucy] was right verballing somebody and it was a
        teacher and [heavy irony and outrage] it was lovely, and if I'd ever
        heard her—she's never done it here—I'd have washed her mouth out

with soap. I couldn't believe it. When she saw me, she stood back and I said, 'I'm amazed. I'm really disappointed in you and I want nothing more to do with you,' and I just walked out... [and] I apologised to the head teacher, and I said, 'I thought you were picking on her and I've seen it for myself now, so how do we get about sorting it out?' She said, 'She'll settle down in time', but it's getting worse.

John: She might just as well be at home for what she's learning at school.

Her parents withdrew Lucy from the school, and after spending months at home, she started at an EBD/MLD school when she was fourteen. Her parents approve of this school because it has boarding places, no boys, and girls can stay there until they are nineteen. Parents in West County often said they were advised that they did not have a choice of school.

Ann said, 'We were told it was the only school she could go to... The LEA say she can't go to [local] school because she'll get picked on ... The teachers too, the doctor said they'll be cruel to her, the other girls just won't understand ... so this is the only school that will deal with her needs.'

It was not clear how much Lucy's reported problems were experienced before special schooling, including seven years in a school for disturbed deaf children, or possibly in response to the schooling and the isolated life at home. When observed at home and school, Lucy appeared to be remarkably patient about the many constraints on her life. Was she actually disturbed? Was she confused? Did she appear not to hear sometimes because she was (perhaps subconsciously) protecting herself from the stream of reproaches (Miller, 1985) and the disturbing contradictions (Laing, 1960) asserted by her mother and, as shown later, by her head teacher? Experts in behaviour might say that teenagers like Lucy deviously make an atypically 'good' impression for strangers. Yet as she had the ability to show these many positive qualities, would it not be logical to provide schooling which emphasises these, instead of places which concentrate on her supposed failings?

Behaviour modification system (BMS)

Lucy's third school uses BMS. Everyone is assessed each week on a five star system, with rewards for five and four star girls, 'normal privileges allowed' for three star, and punishments for two and one star or base line. The headteacher said that no girls are entered for GCSEs, because they would probably fail and would be too stressed. He added that GCSEs, in his view, replaced GCEs, and were only for the '25% or so of children at grammar schools'. He added:

We try to create as stress free an environment as possible [in contrast to] the conflict and abuse and rejection... at home... [The BMS] gives added structure and security for the girls... In a way the girls partly created the system [when asked to suggest rewards and punishments]. There was a massive reaction. Some of the suggestions were quite outrageous, some were very sound. I think some of them have a reasonable sense of fairness... They're very accepting... The girls are happy here... There are clear unambiguous guidelines and they're all told what is acceptable behaviour, and the youngster needs to know 'Cross that line and the consequences will be so and so'... We're constantly monitoring and evaluating and changing the system.

BMS is meant to be a tool for change used for a set period, not indefinitely, and aimed not at perfection but at an achievable standard, with careful assessment before and afterwards. If the target cannot be reached it is supposed to be lowered. If the intended change does not occur the BMS is assessed as too ambitious or as ineffective. Rewards have greater effect than punishments (Ayers *et al.*, 1995). However, it might appear that this school uses the BMS permanently to manage–control rather than to modify–change behaviour in that, for example, the proportion of girls at each star level remains fairly constant. A teacher commented, 'It's ridiculous, every lunch time these girls standing in the entrance hall facing the wall, it obviously doesn't work.' As the head teacher agreed, the ideal of clear penalties can conflict with the ideal of making fair allowances for the context of an action, such as if a girl happens to feel very distressed, or very provoked. He mentioned another contradiction in a system which is 'constantly' changed yet also intended to have 'clear unambiguous guidelines'. Teachers seemed to give unpredictable, arbitrary rewards and punishments. When asked how they applied rules, teachers almost always began, 'It all depends on the individual child,' a form of discipline which allows wide professional discretion.

Girls find the system confusing and oppressive. Their star level depends on how many ticks and crosses they are given each week. 'Someone tells a teacher you've done something and you get a cross, and when you try to say you didn't do it you get another cross, so it's not worth trying.' 'I'm often on one star, I get up a bit and then go down again. I'd rather be on three star, then you can go out of the school with your friend.' 'A cross cancels out a tick but I don't think a tick cancels out a cross.' 'I've been trying all week to get enough ticks to move up a star, but they count them all up today and I won't get enough.' 'They have BMS on the floors [boarding areas] so you never get away from it.' 'If we get one single cross we stay on base for an extra week unless we get eleven ticks. On five star you only have to get one cross to go down, on four you only have to get two crosses, and on three star you have to get ten or more crosses, I think.' Lucy spent twenty minutes describing the BMS.

Lucy: When the teachers shout at you, the girls get so angry they shout back and the teachers don't like it. And if you say something and the teacher shouts and you say, 'Don't shout,' she takes it the wrong way and says, 'Right, you get a cross!' And one teacher said, 'You get a cross,' and the girl turned round and said, 'I haven't done nothing.' The teacher said, 'You're still getting a cross.' It's like, a person wants to go to the toilet. She asks the teacher can she go? The teacher doesn't answer, so they walk off and go to the toilet. And when you get back and the teacher says, 'Right, you get a cross.' And every one thinks it's so stupid, 'cos every time you do something you get a cross for it. We don't like it. We think it's stupid. For the little ones, yes, but the grown ups, no, 'cos I think we should behave ourselves. We should learn without needing this.

Int: 'Cos you know what's good and bad behaviour?

Lucy: Yes.

It may be that the complications in the system increase its power. The girls' uncertainties and constant sense of being watched appear to make them feel cautious, anxious, introspective and self–doubting rather than secure as the head teacher believes. When asked about permitted activities, the typical reply is 'I don't know, you have to ask.' The staff seem to be much less self–conscious than their pupils. Shaking with anger they would shout reprimands, as when a teacher reproved a girl for spreading false accusations about someone. 'Don't you dare tell anyone else! That is one cross, and another for everyone you have told!' The reprimands continued during break time in front of the whole school for several minutes, ensuring that everyone would know about this supposedly private matter. The girl looked down. 'Look at me!' shouted the teacher, glaring at her. The pupils tried to look impassive, but they are in a double bind: if they cry they looked weak and guilty, if they do not they seem hardened impenitents.

There are pressures on all teachers not to question rules or their own authority. These pressures include obligations to apply rules generally and impersonally, to demand conformity partly for reasons of safety, to sustain staff control and collective authority, and to save time and trouble by encouraging pupils' dependence and acceptance of rules. Teachers are also less likely to question or be fully aware of the impact of rules and punishments which serve their convenience, whereas pupils can feel constantly troubled about rules they find oppressive. Interviews and observations indicate that EBD staff rather starkly see the pupils as offenders and themselves as guardians of morality. The staff appear to project all concern about guilt on to the pupils, and speak of their own good intentions, onerous duties and the need for 'firm discipline'.

Katie, aged eleven, who boards at Lucy's school and whose mother had also attended the school, experiences negative kinds of discipline when the staff are drawn into the girls' rows.

Int: So how could the teachers get everyone to be nicer to each other?
Katie: They say, 'If you keep calling her a skiver you'll get a cross'. Miss did that to one girl and she got a cross and she did it again and she had to go the head master and he had a go at her and she did it again and she had to go to base [one star]. When they really wind me or Tracey up, it really winds the staff up, it really makes the staff shout.

Katie was asked several times if there were other ways to help girls to be kinder, and said she would have to think. After a long pause holding her bowed head in her hands, she said she didn't know. Katie only knew other girls at the school, saying, 'No, I haven't got any friends at home, I had one, what was her name? But I haven't seen her for years.' She doubts whether the BMS is effective, 'mostly people are really good or really bad and they are what they normally are.' Thinking back to his school days, her father agreed that the same few are usually punished. He added:

If she didn't go there I don't know where she would go now, I don't think there is anywhere else, she can't go back in mainstream school [having fallen so far behind academically]. I must admit they're dedicated staff. I don't know how they do it. I wouldn't do their job for a pension.

Parents and teachers frequently refer to the heroism of staff who work in EBD schools. Like the zero–sum model of power (Lukes, 1974) which assumes that the more power, say, children have, the less power is left for adults, compliments to the staff imply a similar model for virtue. The more disturbed the students are, the more stable and virtuous their teachers are to tolerate them. While this argument can be logical, its converse is dangerous: the more the staff are identified with virtue, the more their pupils are identified with vice. An unquestioning assumption that the staff are wise and benign would prevent adults from questioning the justice and effectiveness of disciplinary regimes in EBD schools, and encourage unprofessional complacency. Time and energy devoted to mainly ineffectual attempts to control behaviour are then diverted away from education; boring disrupted classes increase the students' sense of being poor learners.

Discipline in East City

Sean is ten. His mother, Bridget, asked for assessment for an SEN statement, a relatively unusual request in East City. From the nursery school onwards, she had been called to the school during the day to answer for Sean's behaviour.

> Bridget:　I'd had loads and loads of meetings which I found intimidating in a way, because I'd go there on my own, I'd have like two teachers, the head and the educational psychologist, and you just feel that you're being told he's naughty ... and they're asking what are you going to do about it? ... and it wasn't until Beverley [voluntary sector worker] came with me, and she said she felt that they kept passing the buck all the time ... she thought that they should be facing a bit more up to their own responsibility for Sean.

Bridget sums up the problem as:

> When he started primary schools there was lots of conflicts between him and teachers, some of them are because he expresses his opinion where it's not wanted. And he questions rules all the time ... Sean certainly has got a problem. I agree that his behaviour isn't as it should be. But I think the way you treat him is definitely something that makes a difference.

What Sean dislikes most about rules is the breaking of a rule of common sense: art is his least favourite lesson because 'they give you something and you have to do writing ... You have to write for English, but we have to do that anyway in English—but in art you shouldn't have to.' According to Bridget, expressing his opinion freely is something to do with his disregard for 'things which you have to go along with', the 'social acceptability' of 'correct behaviour'; for her this particularly means his lack of recognition of child–adult differences—something which her tone suggests she sympathises with.

> Bridget:　They have actually said that Sean has no barrier over where he stands, no barrier as between child and adult, so where with most children there is a line that they draw between us and themselves, like you don't say this to an adult, for Sean there is no barrier, no line ... I mean there has been times when he's been up there [the head teacher's

office] every day, and the headmistress to Sean is just another human
being, another person, to him she's no different from anybody else,
whereas another child might think of them as God.

Sean has an unusually dispassionate view of the punishments for breaking
rules which he cannot see the sense of:

Bridget: When he was very small, he's (I've been very angry at the time)
           he's said to me 'You can smack me if you like,' obviously for him to
           say that, it's a bit off–putting even if you did want to smack him. He's
           quite hard to motivate, but Sheila [support teacher] has got quite good
           ideas and she motivates him in behaviour mainly, with charts and things
           that he fills in hisself and passes to other people, like teachers to fill in,
           to say how he's been, and he has been honest with these charts about
           his behaviour. Perhaps he's not been brilliant everyday, but he does—
           if he has a problem, he acknowledges he has a problem.

Sean and his mother tell the interviewer about the drama club he attends.

Bridget: They have very different kinds of rules to school. There are rules.
           But they have all the do's and don'ts up on the wall in picture form,
           and everyone's equal, the teachers and the pupils are all on the same
           level. And they have 'do not run'.
Sean: Running, yeah. One of the teachers, he rushed over to one of the
           other teachers, and I went, 'You're running', and the teacher was
           running.
Int: And he stopped did he?
Sean: Yeah.
Bridget: There were some problems with his behaviour there, but I think
           the way they dealt with it was much better than at school, because the
           way rules are, you know, nothing is actually 'bad'. That helps him ... I
           like to think that the rules I give Sean generally speaking I do obey
           them myself ... We went to a family consultation unit, we went there
           for weeks and every time we went Sean was a totally different child ...
           And they said that there doesn't seem to be a problem, there's nothing
           for us to do. [But then] things got worse at school and Sean didn't
           want to go back to the consultation unit. We went back and Sean locked
           himself in the toilet during the session. Afterwards Sean told the
           psychologist he didn't want to be there, he didn't think he ought to be
           there, and he thought it was stupid. And that's when the psychologist

said, 'Yes, we have a problem, and Sean needs to come'... Sean doesn't think he has a problem—which is another problem.

Sean's mother thought at first that she needed to remove him from school,

> To get something different that catered for special needs... I thought that it would relieve pressure on me, because they were trained to deal with behaviour problems, so therefore I wouldn't have the telephone calls and things like that which you get from school... But on reflection, I think that it's probably better for Sean that he's at mainstream school... At the time, for me to have sent him to a special school would just be an easy option for me. A lot of pressure that [was] coming from the school, the threat of him being excluded all the time every week wouldn't be there, because it is their job... So I did see it as an easy option... But of course they're not taking children [into the special EBD school] any more, so that option was closed to me.

Like Philip's father, Sean's mother, Sheila his support teacher and his drama teachers treat Sean as a rational person, able to understand, discuss and change his behaviour. On a more abstract level they respect and appeal to his strong sense of justice. To Sean, justice means respecting rules that seem to him fair and logical, and he does well at the drama school which accepts this version. In schools, justice tends to mean obeying adults' authority and rules, whether or not these seem fair to the students. By managing to get Sean to accept this second form of justice to some extent, his teachers help him to behave acceptably in his mainstream class. This is in contrast to the EBD schools which tend to treat questioning students as irrational and disturbed, and denigrate their reasoning which provokes angry responses in people like Sean and Philip. When justice is taken to mean obeying authority, without necessarily understanding or agreeing with it, behaviour becomes a superficial matter of compliance rather than willing, motivated cooperation. Staff attempt to manage students' behaviour by token rewards, like ticks and stars, and by punishments, segregation, controls and deprivations. Sean, Philip and other students we interviewed and observed show how reasoning and respectful care can be effective in treating disturbed and disruptive students.

Expectations and games

Expectations of someone's behaviour can be profoundly influenced by a few simple steps:

reduce the complex person down to a few characteristics, as when all aspects of the students' personalities are seen as evidence of EBD;

assume that their personality is mainly fixed and predictable, rather than changeable and responsive;

ignore the students' own motives and explanations for their behaviour;

isolate the person from the context, such as by separating her behaviour from whatever might have stimulated or provoked it, and the behaviour then easily looks unreasonable.

Staff at Lucy's school tend to think in these ways, which powerfully affect the adults' perceptions of the girls, and the girls' perceptions of themselves and one another. Low expectations can become self–fulfilling prophecies, when students are daily punished for their failings. They have a hopeless sense of 'being bad', rather than of sometimes 'behaving badly', as everyone does at times. Lucy's family spoke of the school her father thought was once a borstal.

Lucy's mother: That school might be for learning difficulties, but it's also for bad behaviour children.

Lucy: They're getting more girls there and they've changed their uniform.

Int: So has it improved?

Lucy: No, 'cos it's for bad behaviour people.

People quickly slip into roles assigned to them, as shown by research in which university students volunteered to play the parts of jailors and prisoners. Planned to last for two weeks, the project was stopped after only 6 days because the researchers were shocked that the 'jailors' had already become so vindictive and the 'prisoners' so helpless, even among people who knew each other as equals (Zimbardo *et al.*, 1973). This readiness to adopt roles can mean not only that pupils feel and behave badly, but also that staff adopt controlling, punitive roles. The anxiety and mistrust typically felt by senior members of institutions (Menzies–Lyth, 1988) are exacerbated when the juniors are officially regarded as disturbed and the purpose of the institution is to contain them (Adorno, 1956; Foucault 1979; Goffman 1968). Some EBD staff are openly cynical, but others believe they are doing difficult work in the best possible way. The main problem lies in systems, in the way EBD schools are created and organised, rather than in teachers' own motives. Punitive people are not bad or exceptional, but are ordinary individuals who work in oppressive settings (Asch, 1956; Sherif, 1966). It is the exceptional person who refuses to join in being punitive, if this has become a routine part of the institution, particularly in relatively isolated ones as special schools tend to be. Further incentives to comply are official endorsement by people in authority and the accepted belief in the inadequate, irrational nature of the person being punished (MacIntyre, 1967). This is why labelling and isolating a group as EBD, or subnormal, can be extremely dangerous. Two common psychological mechanisms enable the staff to support routines which visitors can find shockingly oppressive: these mechanisms are *splitting and projection*, and *transactional triangles*.

Table 2. Common ways of splitting personalities

emotional	rational
disturbed	sane
feeling	thinking
ignorant	informed
inexperienced	experienced
foolish	wise
volatile	stable
weak	strong
dependent	protective
unreliable	reliable
immature	mature
irresponsible	responsible
incompetent	competent

In any relationship, if members of one side are stereotyped by emphasising some aspects of their personality and ignoring other parts, splitting and projection occur. The two groups are set in opposition: them and us, adult and child, normal and disturbed, with positive qualities assigned to one group and negative ones to the other (see table 2). Each quality tends also to be identified with the others in its column; if someone is seen, for example, as ignorant, all other characteristics in the first column also tend to be attributed to that person. This might look irrational, yet the less consciously reasoned these processes are, the more powerfully they can shape attitudes.

In the teacher–pupil dyad there are often clear differences: experience and reason on one side, inexperience and ignorance on the other, though not entirely. Experience and wisdom do not necessarily correlate with age or intelligence; for example, a nurse talked about the profound understanding of life and death which young children with cystic fibrosis who are often absent from school can have (Alderson, 1993). Wisdom can grow through deprivation and adversity. Refugees, children who have experienced abuse or racism often have intense understanding which many adults will never acquire. People in subordinate dependent positions usually know much more about the people with power over them, what pleases or annoys them and the intense effects of rewards and punishments, than the powerful people ever want or need to know about the dependants (Baker Miller, 1976).

By selecting students because of their assumed weaknesses, special schools tend to intensify these supposed differences of strength and weakness. As Lucy explained earlier, independent action which seems sensible to the girls is interpreted as disobedience by the teachers. Teachers at EBD schools mentioned the 'horrendous history' of some of their students, of 'appalling abuse and neglect'. Yet the effect of the school policies might be said to reinforce the helpless victim model in the students, instead of encouraging the confidence and independence they need for self–defence. Even the teachers' accounts of 'building self–esteem' seem to involve an artificial dependence on the teachers' approval, after girls have been 'broken down', rather than confidence gained through taking responsible decisions and actions. The Cinderella complex (Dowling, 1982), of being a helpless victim waiting to be rescued and given happiness, is constantly reinforced by, for example, the insistence that problems must be sorted out by the staff, the infantile reading books, the music lessons on West Side Story and the romantic videos boarders watch during the evenings.

These messages are liable to increase the girls' vulnerability to exploitation and abuse. The EBD schools visited were notable for teachers' negative comments about the students. It may be that the organisation, routines, rules and ethos of these schools attract teachers who believe they should rigidly protect and control the pupils and are unlikely to attract and keep staff who encourage responsible independence. Attention concentrates on attempts to reform the pupils rather than on the schools. Anyone who questions arbitrary rules and punishments is liable to be diverted into manipulative 'games' rather than rational discussion.

These 'games' have been analysed as versions of a negative triangle (Berne, 1966). In the triangle, everyone has the part of victim, persecutor or rescuer. EBD pupils are selected as victims—of their own faulty personalities, of a damaging home life, or of difficulties in mainstream school—or else they have been rejected as persecutors and bullies. Many EBD staff probably begin with high ideals of rescuing helpless pupils from their disastrous personalities and circumstances and helping them to begin a new life. However, EBD students tend to refuse to be rescued or to change or be grateful, and some persecute the staff, who then see themselves as victims. Angry at such ingratitude, some teachers may retaliate by becoming persecutors, partly in the belief that ultimately only punishments will improve behaviour ('break them down to build them up') and that to recreate the students as victims is in their best interests. Some staff and pupils may then try to rescue persecuted pupils, and in doing so they criticise (persecute) the punitive teachers, and in the ensuing rows everyone moves round the triangle again.

Despite rules about no hitting or fighting, it could be argued that in the EBD schools observed there was much covert encouragement of violence. The infantile reading books contained 'funny' stories about strange creatures' fights and wounds. Teachers tended to rage about misdemeanours, to punish rather than mediate. The head teacher's talk one morning ('moral rather than religious', as he called it) consisted of explaining the purpose of each piece of his cricket gear, and the importance of keeping them all in clean good order, so that you are ever ready to 'go out and knock them for six' he concluded, waving his bat. Later that day, when one girl took him at his word, and hit another with a bat she was quickly transformed from persecutor to victim. As a teacher pulled her across the playing fields she shouted, 'You don't understand,' and the teacher shouted back, 'Yes I do, I was bullied at school.' The five–star behaviour management system involved staff in a continual triangular round as they raised or lowered each girl's star level with ticks and crosses through the week. The aim of transactional analysis, the psychology which offers this explanation of relationships, is that by realising the games they are playing, people can escape from the triangle of illusions and relate to each other instead on intimate, honest terms as equals. Otherwise, they remain trapped in negative, damaging relationships by unawareness; part of the trap is that people believe they are taking the best and only course.

However high the ideals of staff to reform their students, these seem to be undermined by assumptions that the students are not fully normal. This is used to justify the psychological game–playing, the harsh regimes in some EBD schools, and the loss of appropriate education to prepare them for independent adult life. The psychological games which distort people's understanding of reality are part of the wider loss of clear identity and purpose in EBD schools which do not share the usual stated purposes of schools—to educate students to enable them to gain qualifications.

The remit and aims of EBD schools: narrow titles and vague aims

The difficulties posed by a system of many different types of selective schools continue to be considered. Despite their specific sounding titles, the aims in the special schools observed were being changed by the national shift towards filling special schools with EBD referrals. Uncertainty in the observed EBD schools about their aims and remit was compounded by educational failure. Terry illustrates the experiences, shared by many of his peers, of lost opportunities. An unusual small unit is described, and we suggest that rather than helping to perpetuate an excluding system by accepting the excluded pupils, the unit would be more effective as a centre working within a large school and helping it to change.

Terry in West County

Terry was interviewed during his final year at school and one year later, when he and his mother Gill spoke despondently about his seven years at a school with a vague MLD/EBD/language remit.

> Gill: I feel so much better now he's left. I was always so anxious, every morning, would he go off in the taxi? He hated school so much. And when he got there, would they phone me about something he's done? Like once he put cling film over the toilet seats. It's such a great relief he's left, we're far happier now. It was a dreadful waste. He only got worse when he was there. He can't even add up two and two.
>
> Terry: But I know if they give the wrong change in a shop.
>
> Gill: Yes you do. And now you're holding down a good job, and the manager is taking an interest in you and trying to teach you maths. But I don't suppose that school will ever get any better. If he was sent there today for the next five years it would be as bad.

One year earlier, Terry's Year 11 class was observed having maths. Some boys shouted, flicked paper and wandered around. There were dirty walls and broken plastic chairs, one bandaged with sellotape. Pictures of autumn were still on the walls in March. The teacher told the class to find protractors, and when someone asked, 'Why sir?' he replied, 'Strangely enough I'm a [pause] um what's that word? I'm a um tee–cher. And tee–chers explain things to people. Go and sit down, and you'll be in for a boot up the backside if you sit there mate.' He then wrote ten examples of obtuse and acute angles on the white board, and told the class to copy them. Three pupils worked hard and carefully. The only girl, Melanie, told the researcher, 'I like maths, and technology. I want to be a designer.' She looked smart and alert, and as if she was a lively, capable, pleasant person. She said she had to leave mainstream school because she was bullied. The boys joked and teased and the teacher alternately reprimanded or teased them.

When some finished the task, no other work was offered. Terry ostentatiously fetched and read a newspaper, slowly turning each page. He then screwed up each sheet and hurled it at the wastepaper bin. The teacher alternately told him to stop doing this and jeered at him for missing the bin. It was not clear whether the teacher thought that his methods would impress a visiting observer, or that they were appropriate for such low ability students. The deputy head described derisive language used by some staff as 'friendly' although the teachers would offer more insults than they would accept from the pupils and they would suddenly change from jokes to anger. Later Terry turned on the radio in his bag, and the amused class watched two large teachers hunt for the source of the sound. When the class went to the geography room they all behaved well with a teacher who spoke quietly and respectfully.

EBD and therapy

Although psychologists assessed and referred students, none worked in the EBD schools observed, and there was no behaviour therapy. Terry attended mainstream school until he was knocked down by a car when he was nine.

Gill: He was in a coma for eight days. They thought he would be a vegetable. His brain swelled up so that the pressure on his skull was very high. He was paralysed on the right side and at first he talked like a robot and we had to carry him and he needed to use a wheel chair. [To Terry] I think you ought to be very proud of how far you have got.

Terry says he is still affected by mood swings. Like two other boys from the school, he sees a psychiatrist at the hospital whom they all, with the head teacher, think 'is useless'.

Gill: But he doesn't provoke Terry, he never sees him lose his temper, so what can he do about it?
Terry: Good thing he doesn't provoke me, I'd give him one [waves his fist].
Gill: We've taken his bedroom door off now but he put his fist through it four times. He gets very violent.
Terry: But I've never hit you, have I?
Gill: Never.
Terry: He [psychiatrist] talks like that bird [budgie]. Don't know who decided I would go. It's just to calm me down.
Int: Do you need to be calmed down?
Terry: Mmm.

Int: And does it calm you down?
Terry: No.
Int: Do you tell the therapist?
[Terry shakes his head.]
Int: What is a session like?
Terry: Rubbish, talks about when I lost my temper. I've been going quite
        a while. I miss school. I'm happy about that. It's at four o'clock on
        Fridays, and the taxi doesn't get back here in time so I take the day off
        school on Fridays. I missed it last couple of weeks 'cos of rock climbing
        and skating, it was worth going in to school then.
[He gets his dog to shake hands with the interviewer.]

It is accepted that adults get depressed or frustrated by their occupation.
Special school teachers said they were very angry, frustrated and exhausted
by their work, and especially at feeling partly helpless, and over–controlled
by government and LEA policy. How did Terry's anger about his school affect
his mood swings?

Terry: I can't spell any more, can't read very well, drawing's all right.
        Got a bad knee and arthritis in my hands. I can still sprint short distances
        then I just fall over. I can walk miles. We went on a sixteen–mile walk
        for Duke of Edinburgh bronze and camped out with the teachers. I got
        thrown out of the territorial army for swearing but it was boring, at
        weekends we'd do assault courses and rifle firing.
Gill: They don't have enough knowledge of head injury. I think Terry's
        the only one there. He doesn't tolerate shouting and rows. They go
        about it by dealing with him, I think they should look at the whole
        situation but they always seem to be at him: 'he's done this' and
        'he's done that'. When they laugh at him, they say he tolerates it much
        better but I say what are you doing about the whole of it? We have
        battles about that all the time.

Terry thought that he did well at first at his new school after the accident,
when it was for 'delicate children'. 'I used to do essays about what I thought
about the school couple of pages long.' His mother quoted a friend who was a
teacher.

Gill: After the accident, she offered to hear him read, and she said he's a
        very bright boy and don't you let anyone tell you any different. The
        problem is they're not holding his concentration and it's their fault.

Terry: I can't concentrate for more than a few minutes now. I don't know why. I just can't. If I'm like enjoying myself, like I'm making a waistcoat every Monday morning, I've just got to sew buttons on, that's all right. But if I can't concentrate, I just do something else instead like be disruptive.

Int: Why?

Terry: 'Cos I can't concentrate and just can't get on with the work.

Int: Some people just sort of sit there quietly.

Terry: I find it difficult though, I'm more active like.

Terry described the change in his school's remit into an MLD/EBD school in these terms.

Terry: It's a lot of mouthy little kids now, spoils it.

Int: Is it mainly for emotional difficulties or physical—body—difficulties?

Terry: Partly that, partly er emotional I think and er [pause].

Int: Learning language?

Terry: Mmm.

Int: Have the teachers changed?

Terry: As you go up the school it's harder, more pressure.

Int: Is that helpful?

Terry: No. I think you should learn at your own speed but people just treat you like by each subject.

Int: In the juniors you might do something all morning? Just get on with it?

Terry: [with enthusiasm] Projects. Like, in science, we're doing this thing with a wire and it has to be a self–propelled marble. Once you start it, it just has to go balanced on its own.

Int: Do you like doing that?

Terry: Yes, it's all right. It's difficult, but it sets your mind.

Int: And you said you liked the school when you first went there it was cushy.

Terry: Kushti.

Int: What's that?

Terry: Good. Wicked.

Int: Oh, very good indeed? You were very pleased to be there?

Terry: Yes.

Recently, exclusions from mainstream schools have been increasing and putting more pressure on all special schools to accept disturbed pupils, increasing their EBD remit. Terry's school, in changing from one for delicate children to vaguely MLD but staffed by several former residential EBD teachers, reflects a national picture. Gill discussed the change of remit.

> Gill: It was totally different. I don't think they should have children with behaviour problems. I know they've got to go somewhere but they're the root of their problems. They spend so much time sorting them out. Terry didn't have behaviour problems until he went to that school, he only had a learning difficulty. Now he's got a behaviour problem which he has therapy for and also for his mood swings which his head injury left him with. Some of the behaviour problems there he started copying them, but they don't seem to deal with it. If it was me, I'd say, 'Right you sit there, sort yourself out and when you have sorted yourself out we'll carry on'. But they don't and I get so cross. He doesn't always do what I say but I am very strict with him. [Terry is much bigger than Gill.] And if I say something, I expect him to do it. It's difficult especially now he's getting older. But if they were like that from the beginning at that school, then surely they wouldn't have those problems when they get older. When he started there, he was happy. But now, they don't seem to know what they're doing half the time. They don't encourage him. I think a lot of problems lie in the school. I'm quite adamant that he can do a lot more than he does there, and they say he can, so why don't they get him to do that?

The lack of staff training and school policy in managing EBD leaves individual staff to use their 'common sense'. Some veer between pity and blame, patience and punishment, then switch to frustrating and goading them to misbehave, as if to test whether they are improving, or to prove that they are not.

EBD schools and the future

Terry's mother, Gill, repeatedly spoke of the importance of a good all–round education, and her regret that she did not have that. Since Terry's injury seven years earlier when she had to leave her job, she has not had secure employment. One purpose of schools is to prepare people for work, to be punctual, co–operative, reliable. Yet if school work seems dull and pointless and the teachers coercive, how does that prepare young people for work, both as new workers and later when they gain some authority over younger ones? Gill and Terry thought the school was not helping his employment prospects.

Gill: I must admit I do go in there blazing guns somewhat ... If they call you 'thick and stupid and dumb dickhead' and all sorts of nasty things, I know it goes on in all schools, but they should do something about it ... There's not enough discipline. They could have detentions, or less break time, or stay in maybe. I don't know. If he's really bad they suspend him for a day, but as he doesn't like going to school anyway he's quite happy.

Terry: I hate school. I don't like it, full stop. If I get a building job, I'll make something and I'll look at it and say, 'sucks school, I built this'.

Other parents described some teachers' unprofessional manner during interviews ('the teachers are loopey, dopey, they act like the kids', 'he speaks to you as if you were something he had scraped off his shoe') which Gill found.

Gill: We had quite big arguments. I'm quite adamant that he can do a lot more than he does there, and this Mr. G [maths teacher] said that in his report. So why doesn't he get him to do that? I mean obviously I don't know him very well...

Int: As a hair dresser, you must have a lot of experience of many people.

Gill: Well yes. You get to know the busybodies and the nosey ones and the curt ones and the ones who are very prim and proper. And he strikes me as being like that, very sort of, when you meet him he sits in the chair like this. [She lies back in chair with one leg bent high across the other and laughs.] And teachers shouldn't sit like that. And with Mr. H [deputy head] sitting with his arm up like this [demonstrates and laughs]. I think, 'What are they up to?' What an example. Really, they should be sitting upright and ready to talk to you, not [in bored off-hand tone] `Oh well if you're going to talk, talk.' That's the impression I get. I think things have got to change.

Pupils and parents repeatedly emphasised the importance to them of being treated as reasonable people, and taken seriously, not as EBD.

Denigration and respect

As if needing to prove their pupils' failings, teachers we observed frequently denigrated and criticised them but seldom praised, even when they worked well. When they were talking about records of achievement, the teacher said:

Teacher: Right, personal development. Has anyone got a bad temper?
[Pause]

Melanie: You could write about being confident.
Teacher: Yes you could put that, because what were you like when you
            came here? [Loud groaning voice] OOOOOOer I can't cope. OOO I
            can't do that, floods of tears all the time, and now look at you. You
            could write something like, 'When I came to this school I was so anxious
            and nervous about everything but now I'm quite confident'—um we'll
            work on how to write that.

—as if he remembered the catch that details about failings were unhelpful in
records of achievement which are meant to support students' applications to
courses and jobs. Melanie might be taken as an example of success at the
school but she raises questions about why she was referred at all to a school
with high bullying rates when she could be so capable, why she needed to stay
for three years, and how she would succeed in future with no qualifications.
Her distress when she arrived at the school may have partly been a response to
being referred there, and to being the only girl in the class.

The teacher read out Gordon's good report from his work experience, but
in a tone of mock reproof and exaggerated surprise at any praise in the report.
He ended, 'A good thing it wasn't worse'. A teacher asked everyone to add up
their ticks after a test, and one boy had 14 out of 14. 'Miss, he's cheating', said
someone. Instead of questioning this obviously unjust accusation, the teacher
replied, 'Well, if he was, he was only cheating against himself'. Perhaps she
did not want to discourage less able ones by praising him but, if so, why publicly
compare their marks? Some teachers stressed the boys' supposed inabilities.
For example, a teacher discussed college entrance.

Teacher: Terry, you better 'phone Mrs. M at the careers office about that
            course you want to do. I'm telling you because you might need some
            special support and it could be helpful to you to know that you've got
            someone to ask for help and support if you need it.
Terry: We haven't got a 'phone.
Teacher: [not hearing his reply] They'll show you round the whole site,
            okay? They'll show you round the whole site. And when they've shown
            you round the whole site, they'll ...

Several teachers had this repetitive style as if they were trying to drive nails
into thick skulls. Later Terry told me that he had already been to the college to
look round and book a place. These examples illustrate numerous interactions
and general trends observed at the school.

One EBD unit in West County which wants to expand launched a funding campaign in the local paper. The unit shares the problem of national charities for disabled people which, in appealing for funds through arousing public pity, denigrate their clients. The unit's appeal to enlarge their 'magic place' used a story about 'Stephen who was bullied back to babyhood'. After bullying at school which 'triggered' his illness, he lay in a fetal position and needed seven months of psychiatric in–patient treatment before being referred to the EBD unit, which gave him considerable help.

The head teacher assured the students' parents that not everyone at the unit is as severely affected as Stephen, but she organised publicity to arouse precisely this kind of fear and pity among local readers. The unit is exceptional in helping all students to take as many GCSEs as they can. Yet it is uncertain how this ethos will continue if the unit doubles in size and moves to the selected remote centre, with all the problems of transport and isolation the other special schools have. The press report contentiously implies that ordinary schools are too dangerous and vicious for a few sensitive pupils who must be rescued from them. It might be said that this ignores the plight of thousands of unhappy mainstream pupils who would also like to be helped. The press message further implicitly denigrates all mainstream students as either bullies or tough nuts who can or should cope. It suggests that this is the 'normal' unalterable state of mainstream schools, perhaps as a reflection of a tough society in which only a vulnerable few cannot cope.

The unit head spoke in a research interview about the lack of psychological expert help for five students who were referred by the LEA that term after attempting suicide. Together with students who had been excluded from local schools, they were changing the original remit of the unit, to be a centre for convalescent and delicate teenagers and occasionally for a pregnant girl. Marian aged fifteen, for example, was slightly injured in a car crash which killed her father and injured her mother and sister five years earlier. She was still thought by psychiatrists to be too distressed to attend ordinary school and was doing very well at the unit. Students warmly praise the unit's humane, respectful and skilled staff in contrast to their rigid ordinary schools. However, in relying on referrals from excluding schools, the unit indirectly enables mainstream schools to sustain intolerant regimes and disruptive exclusions. Rather than starting a larger, more remote centre, the unit could have moved into one of the large secondary schools in the town to achieve these aims:

to be a respite place offering early preventive support before problems become severe;

to help students who have been absent to catch up, and to arrange help for convalescent students with moving around the large campus with their heavy bags;

to be a friendly place for any students to talk on equal terms with concerned adults;

to liaise with the school staff and students to help to make the whole school more humane and civilised.

As other research poignantly shows, such oases are urgently needed in many schools (Prendergast and Forrest, 1997), and they could prevent and resolve far more problems as centres within schools radiating outwards, than by retracting into detached units.

Management and control

In order to convey experiences in EBD schools, we describe examples in some detail: a plan to manage behaviour at the end of the day is followed by examples of how another school tackles the contradiction between encouraging independence and maintaining control and protection by staff.

Punishments continue for months or years with apparently little effect on some pupils. Although their efforts are continually thwarted and hardly seem 'specially' skilled, the staff persist, possibly believing that such lessons can take years to learn. They may believe that, even if it does not correct, punishment works as a deterrent and control that discourages worse behaviours; it is a symbol that the staff have some control, or is an occasion to vent their frustration. Attempts to discuss meanings of difficult behaviour and punishment with EBD teachers met only with irritated dismissal—as busy people they cannot waste time talking about theories. Yet some kind of reasoning must explain and justify their own actions to the staff, and as so much of their activity could be said to be counterproductive, the first way to make it more effective is to examine the rationale of EBD teaching skills.

EBD staff appear to spend much time trying to manage behaviour as if this is the main item on the timetable. A junior class teacher, Mr. Y, spent most of an afternoon away from his class, reorganising a system for the taxi drivers, who complained that they had to wait too long for the pupils after school. The arrangements illustrate the school policy on discipline and use of time, so are reported here in some detail.

Originally, from about 3.20 pm, everyone sat with their coats and bags ready. Classroom assistants came into the classes with the numbers of taxis, such as 3,5,6. The teacher would say, 'Number 3 taxi ones can go', and some while later, 'Number 5 taxi', and so on. Only one or two pupils went for each taxi, so it was not clear why they could not all leave together. It took several minutes for the assistants to reach the classroom and for the pupils to reach the taxis. Mr. Y announced the revised routine at assembly. When he walked into the hall several boys groaned. Mr. Y said, 'Come to see me at break and I'll groan at you, I'm not having people groaning when I come into a room" and he complained about their greeting at length.

His new plan was that everyone would come to the hall at 3.20 (and stop lessons at about 3.15), sit in their taxi group, and then leave together. He went into repeated detail about what they must and must not do and bring with them, and how no one would leave for a single taxi until the entire school was assembled, so that anyone who was late would keep the whole school waiting. He then bent over a cowering girl sitting alone in the front row and using a high fussy voice said, 'And it's no good you forgetting your bag and going back for that, and then seeing you haven't got your coat and going back for that, and then going to get your lunch box. I know you. You'll keep us all waiting, the whole school waiting and you'll...' and so on for some time. The possibility of asking taxi drivers to arrive later, or of the pupils making their own way to the collection point were not mentioned.

Just after 3.20, everyone sat on seven benches, one for each taxi. The benches faced the main exit, so people in rows 2–7 started to step over the benches in front of them, but were stopped by the teachers and made to file out sideways and walk round the benches. If the benches had been set out sideways to the exit, this opportunity for conflict between staff and pupils could have largely been prevented. The bench lay–out, and indeed the whole taxi arrangement like many other instances during the school day, appeared to be designed, consciously or subconsciously, to frustrate and bore the pupils and to create avoidable points of conflict when the staff attempted to show their powers of control. Confrontation over control–obedience issues often seemed to be the teachers' main concern. Did they see these as overt opportunities for 'expert EBD teaching'?

Logically, special education is about responding to learning difficulties. Responding to behaviour belongs more to the disciplines of psychology and psychotherapy, in which teachers are not experts. The 'special' teachers we observed did not seem to be more trained or skilled than many mainstream ones, who were often observed to teach difficult students more effectively.

The teachers' practical difficulties in dealing with misbehaviour linked to their more general uncertainty about the remit of the school.

Deputy head: The main priority is to keep them occupied and supervised. We work on behaviour management. One of the maxims we go by is that if they're busily occupied, purposefully occupied the behaviours will drop away because they haven't got time. If I was doing research I wouldn't come to see Year 11 in the spring term when they misbehave more, in anticipation of exams and leaving school, some of them will be leaving home. And they are demoralised when we start revision and they see how little they know.

'Behaviours' are here implicitly negative, to be replaced by non–behaviours rather than desirable behaviour. Many pupils left at Easter if not before, so that the teacher was writing off almost all their final year: 'they are rather a large class, but luckily they are often off sick.' The aim of keeping students purposefully busy was achieved far more in mainstream schools than in the special schools we observed.

Staff in schools known locally as 'for very difficult children' were reluctant to use the term EBD for their school. For example: 'They are referred primarily for their behaviour but they are mainly MLD.' Terry's deputy head said, 'No we've never been an EBD school,' but was vague when asked about the school's title.

Deputy head: Having a language and communication provision you mean? I think the LEA see it as an important part of the special needs provision. We were discussing about having an autistic contingent, during the redesignation business. I'm very hazy about this.

Conflicting aims: independence versus control
The head teacher of a girls EBD boarding school was asked, 'What is the main purpose of the school?'

Head teacher: However young they are, when they leave school, to prepare each girl socially in their relationships with their parents and their peers, with adults [inaudible passage] to find their way round work experience.
Int: Find their way round?
HT: Find their way round the locality and the town. There's a lot of that in the 24–hour education, access to leisure facilities, to prepare them educationally to find their way around...

The concentrated [boarding] social programme is to er drive towards independence, concerned with their ability to relate towards one another outside of normal classroom, drawing out situations which normal young people, teenagers, experience of trying to get to manage their behaviour, manage their emotions in a less formal way than in the classroom.

However, boarding and the star system of confining punishments mean that the girls have far less chance to have 'normal' and 'less formal' experiences and freedoms. They go to school in minibuses or taxis. Small freedoms which their peers in mainstream take for granted are for them areas of ignorance, in which they are then assumed to need formal teaching. The head teacher explained that the full national curriculum and GCSE courses were too stressful. Instead, teachers saw school work and boarding care as 'therapy' which substituted ordinary academic schooling.

HT: We're kind to them, we look after them, we like them and in a way this cushions their behaviour. We're trying to fill in all the gaps, repair all the damage. However we must make sure they don't become over–protective [at times] we stand back and give her that push.

Staff disagreed over the best balance of protection and independence which threatened their control. They discussed one fifteen–year–old. Some teachers wanted her to stay until she was nineteen: 'she's only a child, she was crying and screwing up her hanky, she's not ready to leave.' The head teacher thought that she should leave because she was disruptive, 'too independent' and so a bad influence on other girls.

Ambivalence about the aims of their schools does not help the pupils to understand or co–operate with them. The girls are not helped to have clear goals or to take personal decisions, in even the smallest things. Self–control, meaning suppression of feeling and impulsive behaviour, seems to be stressed. Teachers' tendencies to see themselves as psychological experts who ought to shape their pupils' personalities have been noted (Mayall, 1997). In EBD schools, this view is still more powerfully assumed. Yet our evidence suggests that, paradoxically, pressures in EBD schools discourage and undermine the students' abilities to behave responsibly. These include everyone's knowledge that the pupils are there because they are seen as disturbed, volatile, untrustworthy. Girls in the EBD boarding school were often exhorted not to trust one another or themselves but to rely in all matters on the discretion of the staff. For example, girls who fetch a pencil or go to look for a book for another girl are reprimanded for 'interfering' and for acting without permission. One girl was reprimanded by a teacher so fiercely that she shook with sobs for about ten minutes while trying to do some maths. At the end of the lesson she was away from the room and had left a crumpled tissue soaked with tears. The teacher told another girl to throw away the tissue, the girl refused, the teacher insisted, they argued for sometime and then the girl picked up the tissue by one corner with an expression of fury and disgust and threw it away. The tissue resembled Desdemona's hanky in Shakespeare's Othello, in the rage, power play and symbolism surrounding it.

When relationships between pupils are discouraged and even pathologised, the main areas in which they could find enjoyment and confidence and demonstrate that they are not wholly 'EBD', such as through friendships, are denied them in ways which contradict one of the main objects of the school— to improve their social relationships. It could be argued that one, perhaps subconscious, motive of the staff appears to be their own anxiety, as if they feel they have to divide and rule, which sets negative models for the girls. The staff punish responsibility as insubordination, and insist on unquestioning obedience, with rules such as 'obey staff instructions at all times'. 'You are treating us as if we are six, we're sixteen' said one girl. Realistic though such protests are, they tend to be heard by teachers as further evidence of silly insulting EBD behaviour, and of the 'need for firmer control for the child's good'. There is seldom clear evidence of improvement in behaviour, partly because there are no clear measures of previous behaviour for comparison. Behaviour is hard to measure in quality and quantity, and there are confounding factors such as learning how to please the staff over a period of time.

Teachers claim to 'build up' self–esteem, by telling students they are doing well, awarding ticks and stars. Yet criteria of being 'good' and doing 'well' are often arbitrary. Teachers differ, and also change their minds, exactly the conditions to increase anxiety and 'learned helplessness' (Seligman, 1975). Self esteem depends, not simply on token rewards, but on experience of actual success and helping others (Cooperman, 1967) which are discouraged in EBD schools.

Nicola, aged fifteen, illustrated a common uncertainty between trusting her own experience and trusting the adults' exhortations.

Int: Do you like this school?
Nicola: No.
Int: Who decided you should come here?
Nicola: My mum.
Int: Do you board?
Nicola: Yes.
Int: Would you rather do that?
Nicola: No I'd rather be at home.
[Her home is quite nearby. We walk over to look at cows in the next field.]
Nicola: We'll go over and see my mum and dad, cows I call them.
Int: What will you do next year? Are you leaving?

Nicola: No, going into the next class I think. You don't have to wear uniform and they give you a dress allowance to spend. There's going to be a meeting to decide where I go. My mum's coming and she'll decide. She'll decide for me, what is best for me, not for anyone else.

She said this as if repeating a school rule from memory, and as if she could not and should not question discrepancies between her own views and the adults' views about her interests. The dress allowance with freedom from having to wear uniform was a decisive factor, and when so many other vital factors about sixteen–plus choices were not discussed with the girls, it could look like a bribe. Elizabeth, aged sixteen, was keen to do a second interview but had to refuse because the head teacher said she was 'not allowed to'. Months later in the 16–19 unit she said, 'I've made the wrong decision in staying.' Yet neither of her parents wanted her to live with them, and she was afraid during the holidays that 'my dad will chuck me out. Don't know where I'll go then.' The isolated boarding school prevented Elizabeth from being able to find independent friends who might advise and support her, and represented only temporary security. The Children Act 1989 requires that all pupils in boarding schools can use telephones in privacy. Elizabeth asked me to use 'the children's phone' to contact her, but the only response was the head teacher's voice on an answer phone.

EBD and inclusive schools

There seem to be two main ways to help students with behavioural difficulties. The special school approach involves adult experts, special teachers, referring psychologists and (sometimes) therapists. It is hard to obtain these resources, and psychologists' enthusiasm to assess rather than to treat problems suggests that the profession lacks confidence in its ability to treat successfully. Psychotherapy is very expensive and lengthy and can only work if the client wants to be treated. Disturbed pupils may well prefer to be educated rather than analysed at school.

Another way is to rethink teacher–pupil relationships, to see students as a resource and to invest time in establishing positive relations between staff and pupils, instead of trying to control negative relations. This is the inclusive schools' approach to behaviour problems, described in this chapter which next discusses why inclusive schools succeed in improving behaviour, where special schools are liable to fail. The two primary schools described here as most effectively reducing behaviour problems share the following approaches: respecting and listening to everyone in the school; taking account of people's personal problems; working on whole school practices which promote positive behaviour and prevent behaviour problems; involving the children, not simply as a problem but as part of the solution.

One school, Seymour, is in East City. The other, Highfield (real name), is on an outer estate of another city and is not part of East City and West County research, but was in a parallel study (Highfield, 1997). Over half the children at both Seymour and Highfield have free school meals, and Seymour is an all–ability range inclusive school. They are described here as unusual examples which give practical answers to questions raised about EBD policies in special and ordinary schools.

Entrance halls and ethos

Entrance halls make very clear statements about the priorities in the school and its attitude towards visitors. They can be welcoming or intimidating, interesting or dull, smart, informal or untidy. They make a crucial first impression of the school. Displays of shields and trophies and rolls of honour celebrate competition and the academic and sporting achievements of a minority. Displays of the students' work again can show only the best or a wide range, can show entirely curriculum work or extra activities as well. Even cramped passage way entrances make dramatic statements in their colouring and displays, welcome signs or negative instructions.

Seymour's entrance hall has seats for visitors, occupied on the days we observed by older women in saris. One window opens on to a tea bar, another on to a small meeting room. Children play in the entrance hall in a pool of coloured plastic balls, and in a small house. Plants, welcome signs in many languages and notices about meetings decorate the walls. The school conveys a sense of welcoming the community, and concern about their comfort and convenience. Parents who arrive to discuss their child's failings are likely to feel less intimidated and defensively hostile.

Highfield has photographs by the front door of all the staff, including the ancillary staff who are so vital to achieving an inclusive school. Along the corridors are photographs of school activities, huge masks worn in city processions, displays of the children's writing and drawings, and books about feelings and relationships. They express the school's concern to enrich each child's self–insight and relationships, and the sense of being a contributor, 'an honest, honourable, informed citizen' of the parish, city, county, country, 'Europe, the world, planet earth and the future'.

Equal opportunities

Schools with well publicised equal opportunity policies might claim to be inclusive. Yet these policies often fail in two main ways: when they exist in theory rather than in practice, and when they exclude quite a large group in the school, the disruptive students. Some statements about official acceptance of all groups on grounds of gender, ethnicity, religion, and ability, state refusal to tolerate bullies. If intolerance is mainly expressed through punishments and exclusion, it can deny equality to some of the most disadvantaged students. It can ignore and increase their difficulties, negate the basic educational principle of responding to problems with reason and not force, and set negative examples of problem–solving to all the students. The policies are then divisive and set up a 'them and us' opposition, the virtuous majority versus the disruptive minority, which is the antithesis of equality. Ironically, teachers' powers to punish and reject mirror the bullies' damaging intimidation and violence. Effective anti–bullying programmes seek to understand other people, respect their viewpoint and work through disagreements with mediation not force (Tattum and Tattum, 1992; Cooper 1993).

Many reasons underlie disruption in schools including violence and difficulties at home, or the frustration, anxiety, shame and boredom of illiteracy. One girl was excluded from three schools. At the time she was in foster care, her foster mother died. She was accepted into Highfield and did well. Another disruptive boy was a refugee who did not know where his parents were. His brother and sister were in another country and from the little contact he had with them he learned that they were being badly treated and he was trying to send money to them. At school he could not concentrate and was threatened with exclusion. There are vital reasons for listening seriously to disturbed children. One example is absconding from children's homes which has been punished with return to the home and isolation. However, it is now recognised that many children ran away for valid reasons, such as to escape from abuse, and the punishment was inappropriate (Lawrenson, 1997). This is not to say that all disruptive students need sympathy, or that all complex individuals should be treated in the same way. Equal opportunities involve allowing for personal differences, which is why reasoned negotiation matters so much.

Unobtrusively, the staff at Seymour bring different children together into pairs and groups, encouraging relationships between many children, rather than reinforcing the exclusive pairs and small groups which children form in most schools. A teacher wrote in a national newspaper an account of how a newly arrived refugee girl became friendly with a pair of best friends, and then became one of the best friends replacing a girl who became very sad and lonely and stopped growing for months (Marlowe, 1997). The teacher was concerned about the sadness of losing friends, but not about how daily events at school can either reinforce competitive, individualistic friendships or help children to enjoy broader more inclusive friendships. Inclusive schools do so through teaching methods and in and out of class activities.

Tidiness

Highfield regards cleaning and tidying as a dignified expression of respect for oneself and other people. During induction weeks, all year 6 children write job descriptions and application letters for posts in the school, including litter busters, librarians, stock keepers, and meal time supervisors' assistants. When helping to run the school and keep it tidy are seen as important responsibilities by everyone, they then leave less mess and litter around. The cleaners and caretaker are respected and, over the years since the positive behaviour approaches were introduced, the once rife vandalism at Highfield has virtually disappeared.

In contrast, in the special EBD schools, cleaning and tidying are used as shameful punishments, to be avoided. The teachers constantly undermine and discourage interactions between the girls, as if they assume that interactions lead to rows. 'Mandy! Don't you dare fetch Sally's tray without her asking you to. She can do it herself, she's not a baby! And you'll only start her off whining again!' The girls often complained about 'interference' after gestures which would be seen as friendly help in other schools.

The close ties between a school's attitudes to tidying and the quality of personal relationships are illustrated in countless tiny examples, such as the two tissues. We have already noted the example at the EBD school, where the teacher used it to demonstrate her power to enforce obedience. The second example occurred at another East City school, when an eight–year–old girl passed a table on which two autistic children had dribbled. Apparently almost instinctively, she fetched a tissue, wiped the table and walked on to work at another table. The gesture illustrated the generous yet taken–for–granted acceptance of difference, and the importance of mutual respect and everyone helping everyone else.

School rules and democracy

In many schools, staff and students together decide the main school rules, though degrees of consultation vary. Some school rules supposedly written by students use oddly adult terms (for example, 'obey staff instructions at all times'). The Seymour rules, chosen by each year group, include: 'Be happy, be friends, don't throw things, look after the books, tidy up when you finish.' Highfield also takes the process of everyone discussing and then 'owning' the agreed rules very seriously. Year 6 learn about conventions, internalising rules, and then decide formally to record only those rules they find hardest to keep. Assertive discipline (Canter and Canter, 1976) includes a series of agreed warnings, careful discussion and a fair hearing of both sides, before using punishments, which are often designed to be positive ways of reinforcing helpful behaviour. The school has a democratic structure of class circle times and the council also meets as a circle time.

Queues, breaks and lunch times: Preventing bullying

Main opportunities for disruption, bullying and disputes occur between lessons, at break times and when crowds line up and move around the school. Lessons often begin acrimoniously with a row about how the class lined up and entered the room. Schools waste hours each week making students line up and wait in queues, start to file off and then have to return to queue up to 'do it properly'. It is then harder for teachers to convince students that they should not waste time in class. Before each session, one EBD school makes everyone go to stand in lines in the playground at the far end of the building, regardless of where they were previously. The staff then walk from the far end to collect students and bring them back to the teaching areas. In small special schools where crowd control is not needed for safety, the military queuing style implies mistrust in the students and belief that enforcing obedience in meaningless routines will improve behaviour. Schools playgrounds bare of play and games equipment incite disruption, especially of boys when they either play team games or are excluded from teams. With nothing else to do, and humiliated by such public rejection, many boys try to show their prowess and hide their shame by joining the game in the only way open to them, by spoiling it. They are then punished for their responses which are largely determined by the context.

At Seymour the staff make great efforts to prevent bullying and other problems from arising. The deputy head said:

> There is so much prevention work on self–esteem, concern for others, and the language we use. The main bullying times are the free break times and we don't have those. We do educate them to be independent and confident. We are preparing the final year ones for secondary and how they can cope with bullying. We don't have any lining up for the whistle and that kind of time wasting. The big danger is that teachers spend all their day on trying to manage and control behaviour, make them be quiet, and wasting all day on this, and never getting on with teaching, say, reading. So much time is spent here on planning the curriculum and use of resources, and preventing disruption and that is very important. The teachers are less tired and frustrated. We spend a lot of time on staff support and working in teams. No teacher can have a bad day, the others won't let her, they are all models to each other they can all observe and learn from each other.

School assemblies once a week are used to encourage everyone.

Every Friday we have a celebration. We celebrate birthdays, and there's lots of noisy happy clapping for children who have worked hard. It's a celebration of the school and it is of relevance to them all from three to eleven. It lasts about twenty minutes because after that some people start to get very noisy.

At Highfield, a community school, pensioners have their lunch in one area of the canteen. Three supervisors, one per seventy children, work in the dining hall, and inside and outside the school. As they say, they cannot possibly see everything that goes on. They rely on children who are their official assistants, as well as the 'guardian angels' appointed to fly to help other children with problems, and the trained peer mediators and house captains who sort out disputes.

Peer support
If Highfield children cannot resolve a problem such as persistent bullying, it is taken to the class circle time. If a child complains about an inter-class dispute, the class ask the offenders to join them to discuss the problem. When an offence is admitted, everyone discusses how it can be stopped and remedied. Future action is agreed with a date to review it. If things have not improved, the problem is taken to the school's council. A boy and girl from each class attend. Some serve for a term, others rotate more frequently. The council members aged from eight years, consult their class about the council agenda and make notes, discuss the business at the council and then report back to their class. Behaviour problems are also referred, after a series of warnings, to the head teacher who spent most of her time dealing with them before the children became involved. Now, she says, she spends little time on behaviour problems.

An example of how fully the children are involved in promoting positive behaviour occurred initially with Peter. The head teacher was going to write her routine letter asking his parents to meet her to discuss how to stop him bullying. The class said they wanted to do this. They wrote a friendly letter inviting his parents to join their circle time. Since then, many parents have agreed and only one father has ever refused. The parents and class discuss the problems and possible causes and solutions, and agree a plan of action. For example, one girl had to 'earn' ninety minutes of good behaviour, anyone could reward her kind or helpful actions with 'minutes'. Her father agreed to buy the class a ninety minute long video they wanted when she reached her total, and he was pleased to hear of the many ways she earned the minutes and everyone seemed to support her. Highfield has avoided exclusions for the past few years and accepts pupils who have been excluded from other schools but who do well at Highfield. Highfield complements the whole school approaches with active personal and social education, lessons, games and activities to enrich the children's understanding of their own and other people's feelings, responses and relationships, with communication and mediation skills. Encouraging children to think and talk about a wide range of feelings can help angry and frustrated ones to adopt more rewarding ways of reacting and relating. East City has in recent years had among the lowest exclusion rates in England, despite not having separate EBD provision, and none were from Seymour.

School structures

The final part of this chapter considers possible reasons why innovations to improve behaviour are more likely to occur and succeed in inclusive rather than in special schools, in the form of table 4 below.

Table 4. Summary of assumptions about EBD underlying school policy and practice

1. Excluding mainstream and special EBD schools	2. Inclusive schools
'Abnormal' covers a wide range of abilities and behaviours.	'Normal' includes almost all abilities and behaviours.
'Abnormal' pupils clearly differ from 'normal' ones	Anyone, staff or students, can have difficult disturbed times.
and should attend separate schools	Helping people in the early stages prevents and reduces disturbance
so that mainstream schools can maintain normal routines	and makes the school a more humane place for everyone
and academic work is not interrupted.	and this promotes academic and personal achievement.
EBD students are disturbed and disruptive	Bad behaviour is a response to context
whatever their context	by a complex person
and they have to be taught how to behave.	who is also capable of positive responses.
The problem is in the pupil	Problems may be in the class and school

who must be changed	and there is always room for improvement
by punishments and firm control. Agents for change are teachers and other expert adults.	through reasoned negotiation. Agents for change are the staff. They work in partnership with students with mutual trust and respect.
EBD students cannot be trusted and must be made to conform to adults' rules.	All students can contribute solutions
They will gain self-esteem when they learn to comply and get token rewards.	and in doing so gain in self–esteem through real achievements
Peer relationships between EBD students must be discouraged to avoid bad influence.	and improved relationships with their peers and teachers.
EBD students fail to learn academically because of emotional problems	Skilful teaching and successful learning are vital aspects of resolving EBD problems
and because they disrupt classes. Low expectations are realistic and prevent stress. Rigorous discipline is essential to correct EBD.	and prevent boredom and frustration. Reasonably high expectations are also vital incentives. Confrontational staff control and tedious routines lead to avoidable disruption and punishments.
Frequent punishments are fair and inevitable.	Rewards work better than punishments.
EBD students are irrational listening to their protests simply undermines staff control which makes students insecure they need firm boundaries determined and enforced by adults.	Disputes require rational mediation and careful listening and negotiation which can increase mutual respect and confidence in a just system.
All mainstream students are on a kind of probation and should be excluded for bad behaviour.	Students need fair discipline and rules which they share in making and in seeing that they are kept.

Stress when they are threatened with exclusion or when they try to reintegrate back into mainstream school is not an excuse for bad behaviour.

Staff correctly assess behaviour

and give appropriate rewards and punishments

which must be accepted by students without question.

Students need to feel liked and accepted in order to be able to succeed
this is encouraged through school policies
which reduce stress and alienation and costly, wasteful exclusions and moves between schools
Behaviour levels, perceptions about them and responses to them vary widely.
It is hard to combine general justice with fairness to each individual
This is why mediation is a crucial part of education in dealing with problems through reason and not force.

Chapter 3

Autism in special and mainstream schools

Barry's mother: Before ... he was locked in his own world.
Int.: So what's made the difference?
Mother: Being with other children.

What kind of schools are most suitable for pupils affected by autism? This chapter reviews professional approaches to autistic spectrum disorder (ASD), looking particularly at the wide range of symptoms and behaviours it is said to represent and the consequent difficulty in presenting a convincing definition. We then present evidence from the two contrasting LEAs, and conclude by discussing theory and policy implications of the evidence.

Professional views of autism

This section reports observations in an autistic unit. It is also informed by visits to schools for severe (SLD) and moderate (MLD) learning difficulties with some pupils with ASD, by interviews and conversations with staff and pupils, and by a seminar for two hundred teachers about ASD.

At the seminar, a community paediatrician described many aspects of the spectrum, qualifying almost all of them with 'may': 'those at the milder end and those with severe learning difficulties may not go through all the stages. Babies may not avoid eye contact. We don't now think that they all do not show affection...' Her cautious and partly hopeful picture of the spectrum perhaps encouraged optimistic, positive approaches, and reasonably high expectations of affected children. However, this broad view could also have the effect of including many more children within the category of ASD.

The paediatrician did not discuss the paradoxes raised in the sets of opposing tendencies: 'He may fail to notice other children or make friends, or he may be indiscriminately friendly and too loud and obtrusive. Language may be very much delayed or he may use very good grammatical structure.' The doctor used interesting epithets: 'Play may be inappropriate.' Can play be that? 'For example, he may put a doll in a cot but this is only imitation and not real pretend play. Dialogue is repeated rather than invented, though there can be original word creations. They have difficulty separating fact from fantasy.' However, for people of all ages, how much do our actions originate in imitation or original (and so possibly 'inappropriate') impulses? How much of our speech is repeated or invented? How far do we see reality devoid of memories and beliefs? To hermeneutic thinkers, 'fact' is partly constituted from 'fantasy', indeed, understandings of disability and of autism are often unrealistic fears. Are differences between autistic and other people ones of degree rather than of kind?

When discussing biological and possibly genetic origins of ASD, and missing parts of the cortex, the doctor added to Wing's (1981; 1997) triad of impairments that they are also

> accompanied by a limited repetitive pattern of activities. The basic impairments can occur in different degrees of severity and the triad of impairments may be shown in many different ways. Education and social environment can have marked effects on a child's happiness and overt behaviour, but the basic impairments remain.

These are central questions for teachers and parents. How intractable are the 'basic impairments'? Does education affect only 'happiness and overt behaviour', so that teachers provide mainly care and control, or can teachers educate these children in similar ways to their peers? And if there are learning difficulties, can they be attributed to autism or to other biological or social factors? In which case, what could or should be unique about teaching ASD pupils? Again, are all these questions specific to ASD children, or do they apply to all children when they are at the limits of their ability or motivation to learn?

The next speaker, a speech therapist, offered many practical ideas on 'helping the child with a social communication disorder in school' and on encouraging social development, language, play skills, learning and self–esteem. She used a less equivocal style.

> ASD is more than a problem with speaking and understanding, it is a communication disorder, in the way the child processes information. They find it harder to extract the central meaning and to focus the message, for example, they see bits of a picture but not the whole, children are keen to point to the spot on my face before saying hello. [The teachers laugh.] It is hard for them to extract any kind of meaning, oral or visual, so that they are confused. They need continuity, limited diet, to wear the same clothes, etc. The more stimulating the environment, the harder it is to cope with. They are more friendly at home or in one–to–one situations than in the class room... They tend to be friendly with younger children. Friends are the biggest issues in

the clinic. They are desperately unhappy about lack of friends. We all
have a duty to offer situations where they can be socially successful.
Free times at school can be the hardest times when they can be very
very vulnerable.

The speech therapist's practical advice included:

Facilitate interaction with other children. Do not allow him/her to opt
out by holding your hand in the playground or dominating one child.
If they cannot cope outside in the playground give special tidying or
sorting jobs. Make dinner time a pleasant experience. Provide the child
with suitable conversation partners. Aim to teach more appropriate
strategies. Help the child to interact in the playground.

On specific teaching techniques, the therapist advised:

If you want him/her to follow a general classroom instruction make
sure you say the child's name *before* you give a the general instruction
to the whole class. Talk slowly in simple sentences and do not bombard
the child with questions. When he/she asks a question make sure you
are responding to his/her intentions rather than just the words he/she
says otherwise you may be on the road to developing repetitive
questioning. Always work from shared practical experience in all
subjects. This is a crucial element of teaching if knowledge is to be
generalised and cannot be over–emphasised.

These are useful techniques, but how much do they apply only to pupils
with ASD and not to all young children? Another set of questions relates to
when adults should allow for a child's limitations, or try to compensate, or to
resist them. Does providing a limited diet or wardrobe reinforce or even
establish rigid, narrow responses? Are difficulties with friendships more marked
in special or in mainstream schools? Are children with ASD viewed more
critically, such as that they 'dominate one child' whereas other children are
assumed to have close friendships?

Then a mother reported how her daughter Jane was integrated into a West
County infant school, concluding that 'School has been the making of her,
and there is not the need for the same level of support in this second year.'

The infant school head teacher confirmed the mother's report and described
the teachers' care and concern about the 'experiment' to integrate Jane, their
planning, anxiety and detailed assessments. There seemed to be a consensus

in the meeting that attendance at mainstream school must be extremely carefully planned, assessed and justified, whereas placement in a special school does not need such scrutiny.

During a research interview, the head teacher of an autistic unit made the following points. Some affected children are not diagnosed until they are aged seven or nine, they 'drift along in school unnoticed'. Ideally special units should be fairly local though not too small, 'so parents do not have to battle to get a place and if possible they will have some choice.' There is growing demand from teachers for courses in teaching pupils with ASD. More parents are 'demanding special places, not just for MLD but for autism or other special problems.' However, she later implied that the demand came from teachers rather than parents.

> [Mainstream infant reception] teachers don't know how to help, they run around wondering what to do. Parents want them to go to local school and have local friends and community. So you can't steer the child to where the expertise is. You hope that there will be more and better assessment.

Children have to travel across the county or into other counties, but the unit was due to expand, and 'three new units are being set up.' The planned units fit the LEA's interpretation of integration policy as the sharing of sites with mainstream schools.

> There is a different range of needs in autism, some have SLD and autism as well. How can mainstream staff cope with that? If a child is in mainstream they may not cope with lessons. *And with integration there has to be some point to their being there* ... In autism there is a wide ability range so we'll have units catering for different ability levels. A lot of these children need residential schooling, because of the stress on the family, a lot need this before eleven. It gets more difficult as time goes on because there is less money, less provision. We can diagnose more of them, and there are more to cope with, some of them who were in mainstream are with us now, they were a bit of a pain, a bit odd, they muddled through school, they were the cleverer and the milder cases, but now we can diagnose them more accurately, identify them in a much more meticulous way, and the parents press for explanations now as to why their child finds life so difficult. And that is different—the parental expectations and demands. Our two classes are basically infant and junior. We mainly do individual programmed

work, we work very flexibly doing different things with different people
in different places. [our emphasis]

I was grateful to the head teacher for her helpful introduction, but puzzled
by some of her comments. Did the demand for special places come mainly
from teachers or parents? What did the children think, for example, about the
very long journeys? If children 'drifted along" in mainstream schools,
especially the `cleverer and the milder cases', did this mean they were doing
fairly well there? Is it economically and geographically viable to provide a
highly specialised range of ASD units? Does the policy of finding a school to
fit the child achieve more than adapting schools to meet a wider range of all
their pupils' needs? If these children need predictable routines, how were these
combined with the flexibility she described? The head teacher made a crucial
remark related to the main question in our research in all the schools: 'What is
the point to their being there?'

An autistic unit

Time
The eighteen pupils were aged from five to eleven. With three teachers and
four classroom assistants the staff–pupil ration was 1:2.5 and there were two
lunchtime supervisors. A notice on the front door said 'No child is allowed in
before 9.15.' Children waited in taxis after a journey of up to an hour or more.
They all entered the narrow hall way to hang up their coats at about 9.20.
Teachers and escorts exchanged wry commiserations about their difficult
charges. By 9.30 they settled into two classrooms. Most children sat at a play
table with one box of equipment and shopping catalogues, waiting to work
with teachers individually or in small groups at a 'work table'. Teachers spent
long periods keeping two detailed books on each child and other records; one
spent half the day doing this. This meant that each child had only brief periods
of actual tuition. Morning break was from 10.20 until 11.00 or 5, 10 or 15
minutes past the hour. Lunch was at 12.00. Lessons and play sessions began at
about 1.20–30 and from 2.30 they cleared up, had juice, looked at books and
went to their taxis by 3.05.

Social relationships and communication
The characteristic peculiarity of gaze never fails to be present ... They
do not make eye contact... they seem to take in things with short
peripheral glances ... The use of language always appears abnormal,
unnatural ... (Asperger, in Frith, 1989)

Given the importance attached to the children's social impairments and their need for special help with social skills, how did the staff address these needs? Usually we were welcomed into schools, but in this unit the staff tended to look at me warily or ignore my attempts to talk to them; a few made me feel like an invisible intruder. Their policy was to teach different pupils each day 'so that they don't get attached to anyone.' We had heard this point made years ago by staff in subnormality hospitals, but did not expect this approach with children who lived with their family and were not maternally deprived. Mainstream primary schools tend to endorse children's attachment to their class teacher and expect younger ones to 'be upset' about a change of teacher.

Annie, aged eight, played in the sand for over an hour at various times. She was deft, careful, imaginative and funny. She called me 'baby' so I called her 'mummy' and she fed me spoons of sand which in turn I fed to her, or we pretended to drink reciprocal cups of sand tea. The staff sat talking together and never remarked on how well she played, invented, and shared the small sand tray and small amount of sand with other children. Martin played at digging for gold and mixing banana milk shakes. Then Nick came up and Martin tried to ward him off by threatening to throw sand at him. The staff quickly intervened, chasing Martin away, 'No we are not having you playing in the sand.' The staff did not notice how Nick then disrupted Annie's play. At last Annie said, 'No we are not having you playing in the sand.' Annie was told off by the teachers, 'You must learn to share the sand.' Later Annie took a dust pan and swept sand off the floor very competently, but no one commented on this.

Like numerous other incidents observed in the unit, this example showed levels of competence, good sense, imagination and sensitive interactions between the children which denied their autistic label. It showed how they were left playing for long periods while the staff attended to other pupils or sat talking together. They frequently discussed the children's limitations, as if they could not hear or understand, for example:

Teacher 1:   She's psychotic.
Teacher 2:   Yes. Not to say obsessive. Oh watch out for Paul! [the only black child in the unit.] Look he's flicking his food, take his knife and fork away.
Lunchtime assistant: [Laughing and with irony] I wonder why? [She gives him a plate of shredded cabbage which he can only eat with his fingers.]
Classroom assistant: Oh look at him, I thought he was getting more civilised. I know you're going to be a naughty little monkey today, I

can feel it in my water. Oh I can't think what's happening to my IQ
today, I'll just go and put my head down the toilet.

Deputy head: Please flush it.

Gary: I'm going to my Dad's on Saturday.

Lunchtime assistant: You're going to a dance?

Gary: No I'm going to my Dad's.

Lunchtime assistant: You're going to a dance?

Gary: No I'm going to my Dad's.

Lunchtime assistant: You're going to a dance?

Gary: I'm going to my Dad's.

Lunchtime assistant: Oh, to your dad's. Well we get it out of you in the
end.

Teacher 1: Eva, don't push Gary. He hasn't hit you—yet. Give Gary his
fruit salad. He's so constipated but the fruit's loosening him up, we
hope. [No one else had fruit. Paul knocked against a teacher who was
wearing a very short skirt.]

Teacher: Well, if I have a hand up my skirt I don't want it to be yours.

The children were hurried to finish their small portions and then all taken to
the toilets at once. The unit smelt of disinfectant though no 'accidents' were
observed during the visits. When they quickly reappeared, several boys had
wet trousers.

At 9.00 am Neil had walked around the grounds with his escort, waiting for
the unit to open. She held one hand and he tried to hold his bag and coat in the
other. Several times she shook his arm when his coat trailed on the ground.
Their relationship, on that day at least, appeared to be fraught and unhappy.
Later in school Neil wept twice, for a long time with many tears. A teacher sat
with him telling him to stop. If children are assumed to be partly or wholly
irrational, if their behaviour is seen as a symptom of a mental disorder rather
than a reasonable response to experience, it can be much harder for the adults
patiently to search for and appreciate meanings, and to engage in close social
relationships. This can be still harder when a child has difficulty with
communication or is unused to being listened to attentively. Neil spent over
two hours a day alone with the escort except for a driver. Parents were concerned
that escorts were untrained and that some disliked their work and their charges.
For some children, transport became such a problem that escorts refused to
take them, and boarding school was recommended.

During the days observed, the staff admonished children who quarrelled,
rather than praising or encouraging friendly contact, though occasionally they
would comment on positive behaviour as 'amazing', 'too good to be true'.

The teachers appeared to expect the children to be unaware of each other, or to make only negative contact, which teachers should be on their guard to prevent, contrary to the speech therapist's advice on helping social interactions. Children at special schools described to us their loneliness at home with no local friends to play with. It is not clear how much loneliness arises from ASD, or from the several ways in which pupils were isolated, or from the effects of adults' expectations of autism.

Sandra, aged eleven, frequently came to sit next to me. She was said to shout at home, but never spoke at school. She was due to go to boarding school. She showed me her school books and read me a story with a mixture of tiny grunts and signs. During break time, she took me to the small shaded area out of the blazing sunshine. Other children sustained eye contact and made friendly overtures. Annie for example, saw me when passing a doorway and moved towards me but was pulled back by the teacher holding her hand who did not look to see the reason for this 'impulsive' movement.

Apart from two apparently disturbed children, Paul and Megan, the rest usually behaved quietly and politely, worked hard when given a task, and talked with me coherently. Yet when a spectrum such as autism is identifiable by so many symptoms, it increases the chances of any behaviour being identified as pathological. For example, usually only one box of equipment was set out per session, with strong restrictions on fetching another box. The unit was very sparsely equipped, especially considering the six–year span some pupils spent there, and this narrow range of activity could be taken to indicate autistic obsession. Alternatively boredom with repeated activity could be taken as attention deficit disorder.

Duncan gave an example of restrained politeness. Clive went to play with the computer, and teachers said how surprised they were at his ability. Perhaps he had a computer at home? They did not address him or ask him. Duncan was very keen to use the computer and, since he was sitting opposite it, every time he looked up could not help seeing it. All the games were brightly coloured, often with sounds such as exploding coconuts or grunting monsters which were hard to ignore. He was told to learn to concentrate on his own work. Each time he asked for a turn, other children were given one. At 11.50, he was allowed near the screen to watch, which he did very patiently. The teacher then slowly sorted out another game deciding whether to have sound, working out how to click the mouse which Clive had done so expertly, and typically doing easy tasks for the children instead of showing them how to do them or checking if they already could. At last Duncan had a short go which he enjoyed greatly, and then gracefully allowed himself to be rushed off to lunch. The literature emphasises the importance of experience and expertise when diagnosing ASD. However, perhaps untrained people such as mainstream pupils, lacking this expertise, would not notice the difference between themselves and the autistic children so much, and would accept them as friends.

Imaginative play

The most general description of social impairments in Autism is lack of empathy ... indifference to other people's distress [and hypothetically] lack of the ability to recognize the existence of other people's minds ... There is abnormal lack of imaginative activity, this refers to absence of pretend play (Frith, 1989).

For about thirty minutes Noel concentrated on playing with plastic blocks and a plastic chicken. He built a tall house of blocks for the chicken and called some blocks eggs. He then made a fox, later called a wolf, out of brown, black and white shapes, in contrast to the bright house. The wolf tried to catch the chicken and push or blow or break down the house and take the eggs. Interested to see Noel's capacity for empathy, I begged in a squeaky 'chicken' voice for help and mercy. Noel was sometimes the fierce wolf and as often the kind rescuer and house maker. At one point he made the chicken die and go to heaven. Noel was fluent and imaginative, funny, sometimes fierce, often kind. He built a car for the chicken to ride in, a bedroom in the house and two bath rooms, and he gave the chicken gentle baths. Later the fierce wolf became a hamster who also died and went to heaven. Other children played imaginatively, like Annie, described earlier. Play tended to be used by staff to fill intervals between formal tuition, and not as a means for teachers to help the children to learn through experience.

Links with other schools

This disturbance results in considerable and very typical difficulties of social integration. In many cases, the failure to be integrated in a social group is the most conspicuous feature ... (Asperger, 1944).

The head teacher commented:

Yes, the LEA has an integration policy and there are a lot of units on mainstream sites, but how much they are integrated is quite individual. They don't make friendships anyway. If they can cope socially that is the hardest part, the lessons are the easy bit. One boy showed he could cope and do well at seven. He is fully integrated now, but no he couldn't have done it at five. It was extremely difficult and he needed help. He has fifteen hours assistance from someone from this unit, and she gradually did integration with him. She works with the class to wean him off her. She's there to meet his needs and also to give the teacher more time so that the others don't suffer.

The LEA policy of integration involved special and mainstream schools sharing sites with visits between the schools. Although 'integration' sessions were listed on special class timetables, they were often cancelled (such as if one teacher was absent despite the still generous staff ratio) or discontinued. The main integration event of the week appeared to be when a few children joined a PE lesson at the SLD school.

The pupils spent break times in a small yard and they would look through the fencing at the other school playgrounds. This was discouraged. 'Don't put your hand through that fence! Either you'll be dragged through one way or you'll drag someone through to this side or there'll be biting.'

Some pupils from the adjacent mainstream schools were supposed to share lunch in the unit 'to provide good role models' said the head teacher, although they did not appear during the observed days. The mixture of special and mainstream schools on one campus had been planned before new heads were appointed who did not encourage integration, so that each school appeared to be as isolated as if there were miles between them.

Learning

The children largely follow their own impulses, regardless of the demands of the environment ... The children are simply not geared towards learning from adults or teacher ... (Asperger, in Frith, 1989).

Annie drew an open grinning mouth with lots of teeth. Later she completed a work sheet, colouring animals and writing in a box how many legs each had. When she finished, a teacher gave her another sheet without checking the first or noticing that it was exactly the same. Annie had filled in the first sheet correctly apart from reasonably saying that the snake had one leg. On the second sheet, she put twenty–seven by the snake and seven by the cat. A teacher said, 'Oh that's silly, a snake can't have twenty–seven legs' and walked past.

Megan was happy, humming most of the morning and writing and drawing on her own. A teacher sat by her to do her dictionary. He looked through shopping catalogues, chose a picture, cut it out, put glue on it, and stuck it on a page. Megan, who seemed to like being active, had to sit watching. At the other work table, a teacher very slowly drew pictures and ruled lines and eventually allowed the watching child to do some simple colouring.

Throughout the next session, two teachers wrote records. Two staff sat with four children, and sorted through squared sheets with some of the squares coloured in patterns. They fitted plastic 100–grid frames over the sheets, and the children were meant to slot the right coloured cube above each coloured square. One teacher said, 'No, that's too hard for Noel, too complicated for him give him this, no this.' They chose a dog design for about twenty cubes. Noel said, 'No, no, too young, that's too young. I'm too old for that.' He did the task quickly and easily. A teacher then spent a long time with pencil and ruler, drawing round squares on large graph paper for him to colour in to match the dog. The teacher put a brown or black mark on each square, as the original sheet showed. Noel protested about having to use these dull colours, though he matched cubes to the colours marked. The teacher sorted out all the browns for another boy, 'so he can't pick the wrong colour even if he wants to.' When a third boy said he did not have enough yellows he was told, 'It doesn't matter, use any colour,' so the object of the lesson was not clear. Noel coloured in his graph paper and wanted to cut it out but was not allowed to. A teacher spent a long time very carefully cutting it out, brushing on glue, pasting it into Noel's book and writing in red ink what the exercise had involved. The teachers exclaimed in surprise that Noel had done the task so well. Like the displays on the wall, most of the work had clearly been done by the teachers.

Therapy

Life is puzzling and unpredictable, so they need security, and protection from loud noises, pain, bright lights such as from wet surfaces. Don't shout because every loud noise will mean to them that you are angry. Provide a certain amount of predictability to reduce anxiety (Leaflet by the LEA and health staff, 1995).

The special school might be expected to be a necessarily quiet, therapeutic haven for children with quasi–medical conditions who find ordinary school too stressful and distracting. However, the unit teachers frequently spoke in loud and angry tones, and there were noisy sessions, especially during the final half hour when everyone was waiting for taxis.

The head teacher said, 'No, we have no psychologist or counsellor for behavioural difficulties. The educational psychologist is supportive but she spends her time doing statements and annual reviews. We are going to start in–unit reviews' involving educational psychologists from the areas where the children live. These plans seemed likely to absorb still more experts' time in costly assessment processes, leaving even less opportunity for psychologists to work in the schools, to learn about the places they recommend, or to help the staff to meet children's psychological needs.

Some sessions were referred to as therapy, such as 'music therapy'. All the children sat on benches to listen to a tape of a woman with a guitar singing action songs. They all seemed to know every highly repetitive song by heart. One song, for example, was:

Now I need to get dressed (4 times)
Please pass me my clothes (4 times)
What shall I put on? (2 times)
Please pass me my pants (4 times)
Thank you for passing me my pants (lots of times)
Now I'll put on my pants (etc.)

Several children had shown few if any odd behaviours through the day but by 2.20 some began to wriggle and wave. If any eighteen children aged five to eleven spent years in this small unit, with the same repeated activities, meagre resources, and long journeys, would they react in similar ways?

Discipline
What is the appropriate treatment for obsessive behaviour—to allow it, to try distraction, or firmly and explicitly to discourage it? The head teacher was asked about discipline.

HT: How long is piece of string? There are a million strategies. It has to be tailored to the child. If there's aggression you look at whether it is frequent or not, find out why, the cause, sit the child by you, separate him for a while, or present orders in a different way, or give them better ways of coping, get them to feel that they can have an influence if they express themselves in a better way. Communication is the major area they don't understand. The world is very confusing for them. You have to make the messages clearer, and see that they learn that they have to get on in the world. There are some rules that they have to keep.

Int: Has the Children Act made any difference?

HT: A little difference. The staff worry about how they and others will interpret it, that you can't touch a child but you can tell a child off. But the Act is not about that at all. I went on a course ... teachers have to stop one child biting another... that is not assault on one child if it is defence of others, though there are grey areas. What is reasonable force and restraint? It can be difficult. We use strategies all the time, some verbal and just a look.

Some teachers used playful threats and actions as a form of discipline. The unusually large deputy head often threatened: 'I'll pick you up.' Toys were

used as tools of control. During break time the deputy head, who often poked
and tickled the children, would lift those who refused to obey orders into a
large plastic barrel stood upright which they could not climb out of. Two
teachers dragged the barrel along with a child trying to walk inside it. When
they saw that his legs had been cut, they debated how to write this in the
`incident book'.

One teacher said disparagingly, 'They do want to do what they like doing,
it's part of autism.' She often ensured that children who wanted to do something
(play with the computer or with lego or in the soft play area) could not, and
children who did not want to do it, had to. Andy wept in the soft play area, he
tried to escape by climbing over the bolted gate but she pushed him back in
twice, and sat there filling in records for twenty–five minutes while he cried.
Nathan was miserable that he could not go in. At times only one child was
allowed in, often looking bored and at a loss, sometimes several went in and
had some fun for a while, though it looked rather odd to see large boys sitting
in there for long periods like over–grown infants.

The staff used mixed approaches to discipline, frequently emphasising
confrontation. During play time, Clive who had lots of energy kept teasing a
teacher who told him not to touch a play barrel. Clive would dart up to touch
the barrel then run off as the teacher approached. 'You run too fast' said the
teacher. Clive looked pleased and raced across the yard then turned for a look
of approval, but the teacher was looking away. After several episodes, the
teacher made Clive sit on an upturned sink for fifteen minutes, where he cried.
Tom cried because he was not allowed to sit on the sink.

David, who read and spoke very well, became more and more agitated about
getting back inside. He had very pale eyes and the intense sunlight appeared
to pain him. He kept asking me, 'How long, how long?' I said, 'Soon ... soon
... soon.' At 10.57 he said, 'It's 10.57', and later 'It's 5 past 11, it's 5 past 11,
let's go on in, let's go in now.' At last the door opened, they all had an extra
high up handle, and a teacher stood holding it and pulling back the almost
frantic David. The teacher called out names from a list of the order in which
pupils were allowed in. A wall notice included notes about each child's worst
behaviours and what the staff should do: 'Speak very firmly, make sure you
are in full control.' 'David is obsessive about time. He needs to be spoken to
and disciplined very firmly. Reward: a book of teacher's choice or toy of his
choice but not clock.' David's name was last on the list to go in. The collective
decisions about discipline among the staff could mean that any teacher who
felt concerned about David's extreme distress need not feel personally
responsible for imposing, or for not questioning, the agreed rule. A teacher
explained: 'We have to let the more reliable ones in first or all hell's let loose

in the class room.' However all the pupils preceded the staff into the classrooms so that the order did not seem relevant. They sat down while the teachers began to sort out the material for that session. Teachers did not appear to prepare work before the sessions began.

The examples have been selected from many similar ones to illustrate general trends in this and other special schools for learning and communication difficulties which we observed. The next section reports observations in inclusive schools.

Challenging change

When he was five, Barry's parents Eileen and Jim were told that he was 'severely autistic'. After she had asked a friend what that meant, Eileen 'went berserk'. Doctors said that 'he would never live an independent life, and he would never achieve nothing. When he leaves school he'll be in a home.' At a local meeting, she heard parents talk about their now grown up children who have to live in residential care. Barry began to attend a special school which was closing gradually. Eileen was very opposed to the closure and felt like 'throttling' anyone who supported it. 'Mainstream school? How's my kid going to fit in? The bullying, the name–calling. That's what we was frightened of.' Barry moved into mainstream with a 'terrific teacher' and is now at a secondary comprehensive school. Now twelve, Barry is cheerful and affectionate, polite and 'you'd think he was a normal child until he tries to talk.' He has lost odd mannerisms he picked up at special school.

> Eileen: I suppose he's got about four or five close–knit friends, but they're not friends who've been told by teachers to be his friends, to look after him. They are his friends because they like him and he likes them. I mean if he didn't like them, he'd soon tell them. But they're his mates because they want to be... I suppose they see him as a normal child, but not exactly the same as them. I know he's my son but he's a likeable boy... he wanted a Liverpool football shirt, which was great for us, which is terrific.
>
> Jim: We haven't put them [new ideas] into his head. It's come from his mates and that.

On classroom assistants, Eileen thinks 'a welfare isn't always enough. I can't expect a welfare to sit with him. So he's got to have a teacher to explain things to him. The geography teacher's really nice.' Some are less helpful or do not like Barry.

Jim: It's the teachers that need educating there, ain't it.

Eileen: You can't blame them, 'cos they was chucked into the-dark
[integration] just as much as I was and Barry was. So maybe in time
they'll get used to him. I could be a welfare and I'm thick as two planks.
I read the Sun. Barry wants the *Guardian*, the *Independent* and the
European, the *Times* and that. What is it? It's the weather map.

Barry is good at geography and French although 'his speech is not brilliant
in English'. Eileen is pleased that Barry is 'a guinea pig,' 'a pioneer' and a
'figure head'.

Other autistic children are lucky that Barry could pave the way and
that he's capable of learning. And we are lucky that our children are
guinea pigs because at least we know that our children will go through
because they've got to be seen to be going through properly. So that's
a bonus for us, our children will always have the best. And even when
they leave school, things will be set up for them I think because they
are the first children to be integrated successfully. If Barry gets into
exams, I should imagine that they're really going to boost him up. They
might put him in [the local paper] to say it really does work especially
seeing as I was [so against integration]. I don't mind because the borough
have proved me wrong [boys and girls] at the school who know him will
learn not to take the mickey and call them all mongos. They've learnt that
you do not do things like that, because they are human people.

He's under pressure all the time, he pushes himself and he's got
teachers behind him pushing him. I think if they're not pushed they're
just going to regress back into their shell, I'd rather he be pushed. ...
Before, he was just confused all the time, and he never showed any
emotion really, did he? He was locked in his own world.

Int: So what's made the difference?

Eileen: Being with the other children.

Their worst moment was 'when he came home crying, because the boy was
taking the mickey out of him. It just pulls at your heart strings. It's bad enough
round here with normal children, they're getting punched and you feel for
them, but our children, they are vulnerable.' Yet his parents think that Barry
does not compare himself with other people, usually he doesn't seem to care
much about being different.

Two inclusive schools: questioning difference

In 1988, the MLD school for pupils with communication disorders closed. All the parents chose to send their children diagnosed as autistic to one resourced mainstream primary school, Morley, which opened a special, all–age class for them. All the children we saw who were profoundly 'uncommunicative' (a problematic term as we shall show) had no speech, or a few single words. Others attend their local school with support.

By 1994, a few children in this category were at Seymour, mentioned in chapter 2. The head teacher here said, 'We don't use the word 'autism', we just see them as children'. They were all fully included in wide–ability peer groups. The head teacher questioned how much avoidance of eye contact and obsession with ritual could be separated from the characteristics of other people, including herself. The children's needs related to their needs as people rather than as 'autistics'. She was concerned that use of the label 'autistic' was inseparable from the way others perceived and related to them as people. She considered that the school should adapt to the pupils and their differences, not the other way round. Two parents had recently requested that their son be assessed by an independent psychologist. The head teacher recounted how the psychologist had shown somewhat autistic tendencies, in his insistence on isolating the boy for the tests, and his reluctance to talk with other pupils who asked him who he was and what he did, or who invited him to join in their activities.

An LEA officer, who once taught in a school for learning difficulties, described how she tried to challenge the theory that autistic behaviour is unalterable, by asking experts to visit Seymour. She would say to them, 'Yes, you can alter it, come and look.' Experts who came to see severely affected children asserted that they could not ever have been autistic. The officer remarked: 'If you constantly alter the diagnosis, expanding it here and restricting it here, you never eliminate the condition: that's a vested interest.' The diagnosis of ASD is political rather than medical, and is about the power to allocate resources, rather than about the difficulty itself. During interviews, several professionals and parents questioned the rationale of putting children with communication difficulties together, and isolating them from articulate children.

At Morley school, fifteen children are allocated to a base room in the centre of the school but are also linked to their peers' class. The base room has a teacher and some classroom assistants, a quiet area with some extra play and learning equipment. Its current teacher is a former MLD school teacher. Each pupils has a different degree of inclusion into their peers' class, between a hundred per cent and twenty per cent of their time.

In the base room I met Aaron, who had just started at the school. I was told that Aaron is brilliant at meccano, so try to show him some interesting things. He is not interested; perhaps he realises that I am not mechanically minded, and my behaviour is at odds with my real self. Why should I expect him to be interested? Eventually he decides to sit on my lap, although he doesn't look at me. The activity of the other boys in the base room appears to be aimless (in contrast to how they appear later in their peer classes). Neville is tinkering vaguely with some plastic objects. The teacher tells me how angry the other children get during school outings on behalf of the autistic children when they are stared or pointed at. In contrast to her former special school, children at Morley can, she feels, copy normal children. At playtime a boy from the group walks and runs on his own, his arms slightly dangling; it looks little different from other boys doing aeroplane impressions. Two infant–age boys spend the whole playtime with another girl, and help her when she wets herself. At the end of playtime, with bells and shouting, each class lines up awaiting orders. The pupils diagnosed as autistic line up separately, and then other pupils take them across to the line belonging to their mainstream class. Some argue about who will have the privilege.

In their mainstream class, Alice and Satnam are already in the room with a classroom assistant working at a table. One of the girls who played with Alice sits at the next table and pats her on the back occasionally. Alice has a story book with a word missing from each sentence. The missing words are on separate pieces of paper, and she has to point to the correct piece. The playtime has illustrated the value to Alice of being able to communicate and the incentives for her to learn. Alice and her parents use flash cards at home, as I did when I visited, and friends from school talk to her on the telephone.

In another mainstream class, Anthony selects names words from flash cards while the rest of the class do a word search. The class teacher works with Anthony while a classroom assistant begins the lesson with the class, and then Anthony is helped by a seven–year–old friend. When the class later prepare for SATs tests, the teacher asks three six–year–olds from the adjacent class to come in to work with Anthony. One of them helps him to do a coloured shape puzzle, and then says to the two other boys, 'Look what Anthony's done.' Anthony completes some of the puzzle on his own though he is foxed by the final two triangles which had me thinking twice, too. Anthony says an occasional word or two, almost like echoes though not entirely. We build a castle with a large lego kit, and then a police boat. I get Anthony to supply me with coloured pieces and then hand them to the friend to set up. Anthony loses interest quickly, but he is very interested in lego people, he keeps picking up and looking at one with a face and a hole at the back. The friend builds a bridge, and Anthony is interested, putting his face on one side to look underneath it, engaging in the kind of personal and symbolic play which autistic people are supposed to be incapable of. He holds very little eye contact but looks towards me relatively frequently.

When she was five, Alice's parents were directed towards a special school, and they moved house into East City, in order to find a mainstream school where Alice would be welcome. (Few people move into East City, except as refugees.) The base room teacher began to ensure that they sat in assembly and at registration with their peer class. Alice's mother gained permission for her to have a packed lunch, when the rest of the class still all had to have the school meal. Alice's mother commented:

> All the things we wanted for Alice, for her to take part in just like anyone else, used to have the same effect. First of all, they thought of the problems it's going to cause—not 'What can Alice get out of it?' It was, 'What sort of disruption it's going to cause to the school?'

There was already a separate gated area of the playground, the 'quiet area'. The lunch time supervisors tended to usher the statemented pupils in there, and although other children went in too, they began to rename it the 'base room playground'.

Alice's mother: The gate was removed when one of the normal kids broke their finger on the hinges. 'All right, what if she gets knocked over? All right, get the cotton wool out, let's wrap her up,' you know.

Father: It's changed now, because I made it very clear to [head teacher], it's not part of our policy, so what are we doing? Alice makes it clear she does not want to be in the base room. She'll bring the card that says 'class 2' to one of the teachers, or she'll go for the door and try to get out of the room. She doesn't spend much time there ... but surely she shouldn't be there at all if she doesn't want to be.

Alice's parents ended separate outings for the statemented pupils by keeping her at home on the outing mornings. 'Every Friday morning used to be the outing day... to the supermarket. I said, "No, that's a special school thing, ten kids and seven teachers traipsing round Asda's to buy two bananas".'

Alice's parents valued 'the willingness to want to be able to communicate,' and criticised the special school she had attended briefly.

Alice's father: She'd been in with a class of kids that don't talk—and how can you learn to talk or communicate when you're in with a class

of kids that can't? If Alice doesn't want to do something she'll let you
know in no uncertain terms—pulling away, making noises, but if she's
doing something she really likes, then she'll show you all the joy. But
with her friends, I think they've got their own communication system,
which is all to do with facial expressions, the way they touch each
other, that sort of thing... She'll spot someone, one of her best friends,
she'll belt up towards them, grab their hands, smile at them, might
make a noise. They'll say 'hello' back, and they'll start chatting to her.

Int: Is it an equal relationship?

Father: I think it is, yeah. The group of kids that choose Alice to be their
friend, they're fairly vulnerable theirselves. Kids that are very shy, kids
that have problems in making relationships, kids that are very nervous,
a lot of kids that don't want to be at school, that sort of child, yeah?
Alice doesn't make the demands that a lot of kids in the school make
on them you know, 'You haven't got your Reebok trainers on' or 'Ooer,
you look weird today, what you wearing?'

Int: Is this just non–threatening, or does Alice offer something positive?

Father: Alice does give a lot back. She's really warm, she shows other
kids that she's really happy to be in their company. At the end of the
summer term there are all these kids in tears... A big strapping lad was
crying because Alice is leaving. In particular for the boys, they've
become such nice, caring kids, without mothering Alice. They're
actually able to show a kid from the opposite sex that they care... The
kids accept that, and there is this boy Peter who's cuddling Alice in the
playground, and nobody's laughing at him.

These articulate but not educationally privileged parents could exert
influences based on their observations of the school. It would be harder for
them to be so aware and involved if Alice were at a special school further
away. Alice's head teacher emphasised his own influence on changes in the
school, though he acknowledged the part played by families. He said that the
disabled children gave 'power' to the rest, signifying confidence and maturity.
Class teachers' attitudes towards including the statemented children in their
own class differed markedly, and it was not clear how potentially unjust
differences in teachers' practices were addressed. Staff in the base room, as in
special schools we observed, attended to one child at a time, while others
meandered aimlessly and they all appeared 'autistic'. In contrast, in their peer
class there were at least minimal interactions with the other children, and our
adult interviewees insisted that, in time, their behaviour showed the influence
of their peers.

I followed Satnam and Wayne into year seven at a local comprehensive where they spent all their time with their peer class. A classroom assistant described how he sometimes took them:

> to our little room we go up to, we've got a mini library. Some of the other students say, 'Please sir, please miss, can we come up with you?' And they come up and join in with them ... although basically the idea of it is a haven or sanctuary for people who need it at a time of stress.

The assistant described his worst moment:

> when Satnam threw his first major wobbly. And it was bad. I took him out of the classroom initially and they actually had teachers coming out of their classroom from the second storey to find out what the screaming was about.

He went on to describe how this recurring event is no longer remarked upon. He also said that pupils will

> come across and say, 'Can we borrow your rubber?' and this is what they use as excuses just to make them feel at home. They really go out of their way to make them feel part of it.

Chapter 4

LEARNING DIFFICULTIES IN CONTEXT

George's Father: I think one of the main problems is public attitudes to mental handicap. Traditionally it's been treated with fear and mystery. Before we can have integration we've got to have a lot of public education before the mentally handicapped can be acceptable in mainstream schools. When it's not done properly it fails, mainly because sufficient money will not be made available. None of the special services that are required will be in place or they will be so watered down over a very wide area that they will be quite useless, and probably aggravate the very problems they're there to solve. I'm totally opposed to integration into mainstream.

Vishal's brother: Well of course that [segregation] was what happened to us at first, so I knew what the feeling is like when someone says, 'Well you're not allowed in this room, like forever.' Then you get that feeling of being left behind, and then suddenly you hear that things are changing and you can see a window opening, and it's been really good for us.

In West County Matthew illustrates the experience, common for families, of education and health professionals offering 'special' help and drawing children away from mainstream preschools and schools, from chances to play and learn with ordinary children into repetitive routines and small–step learning which help to confirm low expectations. We discuss the sense of purpose or 'destination', as Vishal's brother will say later, of SLD schools, and the glass wall of segregation they construct. The remit of schools for learning difficulties and the very wide ability range they cover are considered, with questions about what makes them special, and examples of science, art and music lessons in a school for 'language and communication difficulties'. In East City, we report mainstream secondary life for Vishal who has Down's syndrome, and concepts of normality and disability. We also look at Tracey's 'backwardness' and describe an individual learning programme and a differentiated science lesson. An inclusive primary school is described, and Ben is reported doing a GCSE course.

Matthew: 'Just for us'

Matthew's mother Joanna is speaking when Matthew is fourteen years old. He has severe tuberous sclerosis and epilepsy, and attends an SLD school. Many of the points she makes were also made by other parents.

> Joanna: Dr. B, the paediatrician, painted a very gloomy picture [fourteen years ago], awful at the time, he painted the worst picture. Matthew has done so much better than we expected, every new thing he does we're very happy and pleased. We're not disappointed that he won't read or write because we don't expect it. We were very lucky to have portage with Miss R, a paediatric nursing officer. She'd set very small easy tasks each week. She'd come into our home for an hour or more and often witnessed fits he'd never have at hospital. She'd liaise with Dr. B, and he'd say increase the tablets...
>
> I think normal children will do it [learn] themselves when they're ready, but with slow learners you've got to help them and encourage them—well, they might do it in their own time but you've got to feel that you're giving them some help.
>
> For years he wouldn't look at you, no eye contact, he'd look only briefly at objects. She'd bring toys for him to look at, a musical potty, ways of rewarding him, sometimes they worked and sometimes not... She organised that he go to a speech therapy clinic, and a small playgroup at the hospital when I could leave him and go shopping, and she suggested a wonderful music therapist. I think she taught him to speak by singing repeatedly the same songs. I stayed with him then, she said she couldn't cope on her own.
>
> He went to a small playgroup locally for six months with normal children. He was the only disabled one they had, he was a bit disruptive at times. Then, when he was three, he went to the nursery at the SLD school. It was much more geared to him, small groups with more individual attention, more staff to help with toilet training and feeding. The teacher was marvellous about the potty training. I couldn't believe that he would ever be toilet trained. But when he was about four or five he did learn. I think it was my husband really. He'd say, 'This is what you do, watch daddy, Matthew try and do it,' and one day he just did it.

Like many parents, Joanna praised the staff but qualified this by her report, so that their actual contribution is uncertain and reality is left suspended between the lines: were all the years of potty training worthwhile and effective when Matthew could have been enjoying the stimulating play that he needed?

Joanna: Matthew enjoys going out and doing things. He doesn't watch
much TV, but he likes his videos, Postman Pat and Famous Five, he
knows them off by heart. His understanding is getting better all the
time, better than his speech. He's only had speech therapy for six to
twelve months and his speech is clear now. Recently he's started saying
something else if you can't understand what he's saying. He's quite
patient, though he gets cross such as if he can't get a sock on. He
doesn't mind if we take a long time to understand his words.

The one big thing is that Matthew doesn't go out and play. We have
to entertain him all the time, and we have to take him everywhere.
He's got no road sense and he'd just wander off. The local children
hardly play with him round here, but one or two are good near his
nanny's house, one ten–year–old plays with him in the garden, and a
few come in to play, very simple card games, for instance. We go out a
lot to friends and relations and we never leave him out. He's got to be
fairly socially acceptable for us to take him out to restaurants. We expect
him to behave himself. I don't take him shopping, he'd run off.
Occasionally we go to the supermarket and they sometimes take him
at school. He makes cup–a–soup at school and he hands round biscuits
and orange to the rest of his group and has his at the end, and he's
pleased when he can do this. He doesn't do reading or writing, they
use signing at school but because he can speak he never really signs.
They have music therapy, individual tuition twice a week. He enjoys
football, I'd like to see that more at school. He goes to one girls'
[mainstream] school once a week for cooking, he enjoys that. He gets
on well with fourteen, fifteen and sixteen–year–olds, he might take
more notice of them than of adults.

Int: So you are pleased with his school?

Joanna: He's in quite a large class of twelve, and he definitely needs
individual attention. If there's a free room they can take a child away
for one–to–one. Sometimes you wonder why they're doing national
curriculum science, but when it's broken down to his level it's okay.
Maths is matching colour numbers; he can count, but he doesn't
understand numbers. Sometimes I feel they should teach him more to
wash himself and dress himself. They help him along the way, but now
it's more the subjects, whereas the feeling was years ago that if they
just made them socially acceptable and maybe they knew how to dress
themselves that was enough If only school would teach them self–
care. I think he is able to do these things, but I can't get him to stop

relying on me. I need an expert to come and help us to move on a bit, like the portage idea of steps of progress but for dressing and washing.

When shopping, many small steps and bits of knowledge relate to a coherent whole. Yet as Joanna and other parents recount, the special school system draws pupils away from mainstream society. Moving from a playgroup into an SLD nursery prevents Matthew from learning how to be one of a group of 'ordinary' children who go shopping or use public transport or play football. Joanna and Matthew join in several local Mencap activities, clubs and outings, and the town leisure centre is booked once a month and the swimming pool once a week 'just for us'.

A sense of purpose?

When the whole day is taken up with repeated small tasks, it is harder to have a sense of purpose or plan. Matthew's SLD school has a very pleasant atmosphere, the staff are generally calm and kind, the rooms have attractive displays, the staff worked hard to raise funds for a beautiful sensory room, and talk in the staff room is positive and affectionately respectful of the students. As our aim was to understand the students' views, we would observe individuals. In the SLD junior school Simon, aged eight, starts his school day with a lengthy settling down time while buses and taxis arrive. Quiet music plays, a child is massaged, Simon sits waiting. About ten minutes is spent moving the class to sit together and gaining their attention. The teacher says good morning to each one and slowly goes through the register and lunch list. Then they talk for a few minutes about the weather and what they are going to do, the teacher saying and signing 'And today the colour of the sky is ...?' for them to complete. Stacy's gaze wanders around the room, although occasionally she looks very interested in the session. Someone says that she is going to the dentist this morning; another girl opens her mouth wide and says 'aaagh' and is praised. Stacy stops looking vacant and copies the girl; a classroom assistant says, 'Don't put your fingers in your mouth.'

Then the staff put a few books and toys on the tables. Valerie, aged nine, talks to a classroom assistant about her gran's troublesome boyfriends while the staff stand by the kettle, mainly talking to one another and shushing children who try to interrupt them. After thirty minutes Simon fetches a tray and starts pouring lentils. A classroom assistant removes the tray, saying 'It's time for your orange juice.' The classroom assistants spend fifteen minutes brewing tea and making toast, then serve the juice. The children eat and are wiped clean. Simon fetches the tray again. Hearing the sound of the lentils, an assistant says, 'I can't stand that noise any longer' and removes the tray. Nigel, a lively

boy, roams the classroom; the staff worry about this, because they feel they
must keep the less mobile children in their chairs. Later, during lunch, Nigel
helps other children and pours water for them. He watches a boy trying to peel
an orange before holding the plate steady for him then cutting it into quarters.
Children tend to be left where they are placed, and they gain the adults' attention
when they show boredom and frustration.

After 10.20 the staff begin to take some of the children to a swimming pool
a long bus ride away. The five most disabled children go to the school's own
hydrotherapy pool. For nearly two hours, two assistants change them and one
holds them individually in the pool for a few minutes with long gaps in between
dips while the next child is changed. 'It's funny, I don't like kids,' one remarks,
'but I like working here.' The silent passive children seem like patients or
dolls, with nursing staff rather than teachers.

The staff talk about the children. 'Fay has a progressive disease, she's going
to die soon and we try to make her days as good as we can, give her a good
quality of life. Her mother dresses her beautifully.' Tina looks delighted when
she is lowered into the pool and very upset later when a boy keeps pulling at
her arm. 'Tina's parents are looking for a school where she can live all year
round. They work abroad.' I ask the staff about the main aims of their work.
'To make their childhood as happy as possible. To prepare them for adult life.
To develop their potential. Like Superman [the actor who has been paralysed]
you'd do your very best for him, it's the same with these when they're born,
we should do our best for them.' Then they talk about Nicholas (whom we
encountered in chapter 2) who has 'destroyed' a classroom and been excluded
for months from his MLD school. He will come to the SLD school. 'No one
else will take him. If he doesn't fit in here he'll have to go to residential school
where he can be properly managed. There used to be big places where they
were sedated for the rest of their lives, but these have gone now. I suppose now
there are small places to go to.'

In the afternoon, some children do PE 'integrated' with two visitors from
an autistic unit. The 'more sensory children' do 'body awareness'; the staff
rub parts of the body with a sponge or a scourer, and do movements and songs.
By the end they all lie very still on the carpet while Indian music plays. Then
slowly they begin to move and whisper. A classroom assistant said, 'I've spent
months teaching them to relax and stop fidgeting, and it was so good for Stacy's
mother to know she can do this.' After they had talked as a group about what
they had done, five children went to the sensory room to lie gazing at the
moving lights. In the windowless room with fibre optic glitter in the carpet
and large transparent tubes in which bubbles rise and fall, projected images of
clouds or fireworks on the walls appear at the touch of a knob.

When taught in small steps, as considered in chapter 1, students have to work out how they apply in real life, and to invent missing links. This is illustrated by a session on money in the unit for more able students in the fifteen to nineteen age–range at Matthew's school. Staff had spent most of Friday afternoon making tea and completing plans and records ('We're exhausted at the end of the week'); now it is Monday morning, and it begins slowly ('We're exhausted after the weekend'). The money session concerns recognizing and matching coins. Jars of one, two, five and ten pence pieces are set out, with photocopied sheets showing rows of coins. The students are asked to put real coins over the pictured ones. The pictures are not only black and white but smaller than the actual sizes. It is impossible to fit the metal coins on to the paper shapes. To make any sense of matching, the students would have to understand the purpose and approximate value of the coins. Some seem to have no idea about matching, but one, Andy, easily calculates the sum of all the coins. Despite this difference, later everyone has the same maths cards on which to write the money in words and figures. The next lesson is English but the teacher says that instead some of them can clean her car to earn money towards their class holiday while the others can do what they like; some play snooker, expertly.

The glass wall

A main purpose of schools is to prepare students for life 'in the adult world'. However, their assumed future seemed to be to accept being secluded at the edge of society, rather than to expect to be a contributing member. The 15–19 unit is in the grounds of the neighbouring comprehensive. Grey blinds remain closed over every window, and the limited equipment is kept in grey trays; walls and paintwork are soft grey. The hut is near tennis courts, a field and a yard. A few boys from the mainstream school come near the hut, and they play football with a small blue ball on the field. Lisa who has Down's syndrome and Alan, the two most outgoing ones in the unit, play football with a tennis ball nearby in the yard. Sometimes the balls move across into the other game. Lisa is very good at returning the blue ball with strong accurate kicks: she could easily join in the boys' games. There is a little hesitant overlap at times. The balls look like poignant symbols of attempts at inclusion that are constantly returned as if they are intruders.

It is as if an invisible thick glass wall separated the 'special' from the ordinary students, which no one could pass through. How can older teenagers reintegrate, when so much adult effort has been and still is devoted to keeping them apart? The timetable on the wall lists 'integration' with the next–door comprehensive at lunch and at another girls' school for some lessons, but staff say they no longer do any of this. 'When we went over for lunch we'd sit at a separate table. Some of the girls were good and they'd come over and sit with us sometimes ... No, it's not our job to encourage contact. I couldn't, I'm just an assistant. The new heads at the main schools aren't keen. It would be nice if we had some contact, but it just doesn't seem to happen. I don't know any of the teachers.'

The remit of schools for learning difficulties

A complication in the SLD school's remit is that it includes very immobile, dependent pupils and aggressive, challenging ones rejected from MLD schools. The deputy head was asked about the latter.

> Deputy head: We have some children whose challenging behaviour is too challenging, so we accept the risk that involves other pupils, some are even defenceless. It's a balance between those children's needs and the whole. And if it comes to a time when it's affecting their education we would have to see how that could be changed. There are limits to the modifications you can make to the curriculum and resourcing and staffing. Whoever is responsible for that child would have to decide what is the provision of education that is best for that child's needs ... It's all justifying the expense, the resources. If the educational provision needs to be twenty–four hours, you are talking about someone with exceptionally difficult needs, they are going to respond to a twenty–four hour provision as opposed to a day school. We wouldn't want anyone to leave unless we felt they were going somewhere that was better.

Asked how he knew it was better, he replied that it is not possible to follow up these pupils to see what happens in boarding school. There is clearly a difficulty in that no one can be sure that boarding will work, or even that it will be better. If someone is unhappy and doing badly at day school, boarding school could simply be more of the same and leave them still more unhappy.

> Int: So the range of children here means that you have quite a mix of ability in each class?
> DH: We don't segregate pupils at all.
> Int: So, in a way, you are teaching a wide ability range?
> DH: The whole of SLD in each class.
> Int: And there seems to be a wide age range.
> DH: Each class covers two years and we do try to group by age, but in a

small school that's quite difficult because you get bulges of certain ages. So as numbers increased we tended to—we have looked at sizes of classes and tried to fit pupils in their age group where the class is able to accommodate them, and that has led to rather large classes. So for a certain period of the curriculum we do regroup across classes, where it is more ability based, things like using the swimming pool in the community or the hydrotherapy pool, different types of PE activity, and when certain pupils need more staff support than others.

Here, ability seems to mean mobility rather than educational ability. As parents also commented about SLD and MLD schools, two–year groupings could mean children repeating a whole year of lessons, though at SLD schools there seemed to be little difference between lessons for some two–year–olds and some nineteen–year–olds. Parents were concerned about class sizes.

Joanna: We visited another school and were amazed at the small classes. Then, because we'd made a fuss, the headmistress then invented the smallest class, four children, and Matthew was much better after that. But then he went on to a bigger class but with fewer of the very disruptive ones. It's so difficult when there's such a wide range; some can read and write and others can't do anything. They might do very simple science that maybe would benefit some in the class, and the others just have to go along with it. His statement at five years said he needs to be at SLD school full–time. All along, I've always said he needs to be in a small class with a lot of individual help. It's no good being one of many in the class, just left to get on with it ... He wouldn't get on with it, he'd just do his choice.

If organisation is inflexible and teaching not differentiated, students miss opportunities. Stacy shows how they can fall between types of provision when schools try to be over–specialist. Aged eleven, she uses a wheelchair and communicates mainly by little cries, though she said 'more' when the researcher read her a story. Her classroom assistant, Kate, said:

I've been one–to–one with Stacy for three years, fifteen hours a week, though it's very hard to find the time with PE one morning and swimming two mornings a week. She is very bright and could do a lot more. She had the chance to go to the local physical disabilities school, but all the juniors have to board [this is not actually the case] and her parents want her to live at home. Now we go one morning a week and

we enjoy it, she's benefited from being with the other children and
seeing the equipment, like machines they can use with their chins.
That school is now taking more PMLD children, but they [staff] fall
apart at things we take for granted, like when a girl puts two fingers
down her throat. It would be better for Stacy to be there, but it's too
late. *She's fallen too far behind and she can't cope with the structured
day.* She could do the English and the maths, but not science. It's hard
to communicate those kinds of ideas, she's too easily distracted and
has little concentration, though *it's improved a lot since she's been
going there.* She's staying at the [SLD] secondary school here, though
I feel a lot of her potential will be lost. She's too bright for this school,
but she's not up to the PH school. They say they'd only have her if they
could make up a class of six children like her. She doesn't really fit
into any school. We need special schools because in mainstream it's
all right for the top ones, they teach themselves, and the bottom ones
get help but the middle ones miss out. It's unfair to have them all
together. And with autistic ones, some are very bright and some are
SLD and you need different schools for them.

As our emphases indicate, Kate's views raise questions about how much
the SLD school holds students back, reinforcing and even creating learning
difficulties; this contrasts strongly with the inclusive schools described later.

How are schools for learning difficulties special?

Teachers acknowledged that MLD or SLD classes included students with a
very wide variety of abilities and needs. They were often vague about the
precise reasons for referral to their school.

Int: Are the school's entry criteria linked to intelligence?
Deputy head: Ooooh [pause] you know which button to push don't you.
        No it is not. There is no such thing as measurable intelligence [said
        loudly and firmly].
Int: Oh ... Yes?
DH: No, that's not quite true. Er...
Int: I agree with you that there isn't, but is entry linked with ability to do
        IQ tests?
DH: No no.
Int: Not at all?
DH: [loudly] NO.
Int: So you have a wide range of ability here?

DH: Um, I don't think so actually, because I suppose one of the criteria revolves around...it's to do with thinking of children's learning potential and thinking perhaps of the speed with which they can learn rather than giving them a number which might appear to be just a limit on the children. I suppose the definition of the children is to do with a language impairment which impairs either their ability to access material or their ability to output it in an appropriate way, but who have to all intents and purposes a fairly, in inverted commas, 'normal' range of ability in processing information.

The actual 'language and communication provision' was unclear, as the deputy head explained.

DH: Although we had worked very hard, we hadn't really looked at any kind of language work which is a nonsense in a language school. OFSTED pointed that out to us.

Int: How did you look more at language?

DH: Well, we ran an internal course, the staff...didn't have much knowledge of language. Some of the staff are from mainstream, the majority are from EBD schools ... The course was done at very short notice and the content was very thorough. We looked at the development of language, at social language, everything from body language to things like not interrupting, um, being able to, er what we tried to investigate was ways of improving memory, um, we looked at the whole range but in fact nothing seemed to hang together in the course ... [We had] a special needs lecturer ... My understanding was that she knew something about language, um I'm not convinced that she actually did any better a job than I could have done and I knew nothing about language.

Int: Do you think there is a valuable expert body of knowledge about this or do you think a lot of it is common sense?

DH: I believe when I did my last diploma in special needs I actually looked at the language assessment mediation tool [lists specialist terms] and frankly the vast majority of language development is so complex I don't believe that you could apply common sense to it. [He discusses 'allocating a sort of language age like a reading age'.] Now I accept those sorts of things are, er valuable perhaps in terms of giving some kind of baseline and then something to progress from, so perhaps you've got a notional level when you start, so that you know whether you're improving a child's language.

Int: Who's that valuable for?

DH: Well that's valuable for the teacher to know whether you are, what you are doing is creating an improvement.

Int: And is there a set of exercises or anything to go with it?

DH: Well no, there's nothing like that, you see language is a very, is a terribly difficult thing to put your finger on because it doesn't develop or doesn't appear to develop in any kind of linear way. I mean if you look at a child learning to add in maths, um you start with er perhaps two numbers, two digits that add up...

Int: By putting your finger on the stages, does it actually facilitate the process or does it complicate it?

DH: No, I think in many ways it muddies it and confuses the issue.

Int: And do the children actually benefit from any of these strategies?

DH: Um...

Int: Is there any evidence that they do?

DH: Er no, not that I know of. You see, I'm not a language specialist.

Int: So if this is a school for language, what does this school offer that the children wouldn't receive at their local school?

DH: Right, well I think the main, I think I can answer that in several ways. Let me get my thoughts together.

His answer was to describe a boy's perceived needs:

DH: One boy has quite a good understanding of science. His work is really focused, and he is by far and away ahead of the rest of the group. I wanted him to do GCSE science and...it would be virtually impossible for me to give him any kind of individual help towards doing GCSE. So I arranged for him to go to a local [secondary modern] school for a daily lesson and we would pay for a notional one day a week and transport costs just up the road and back in the classroom assistant's car, the assistant stayed with him in the lesson. In the first three weeks I acted as the assistant because I wanted to see what was going to go on.

After I withdrew from being the assistant he was unable to carry on. The reason very simply was that I found myself translating for him what had been said. In other words I was actually taking the input the mainstream teacher was giving to the whole class and I was having to break it down and translate it for this boy to access. The translation took several forms, I suppose. I sat with or near him, I was able to rephrase what had been said, I was able to put in substitute words which I knew the boy would be able to understand and simplify the concept and to explain with a drawing. Without that level of support he just failed. Simple as that ... Science appears to be such a specialist subject that no one, certainly not the assistant, was able to explain to him in a different way. It got to the stage where he was starting to misbehave quite seriously because he was starting to feel frustrated and that it wasn't working, and so we ended it then. So, er, from that I hope I can pull out the main things we do, I feel, are to are to make the work accessible by using language the children can access and by being prepared, because of the size of classes, being able to rephrase things several times.

The above example raises questions about how much the other science students understood the lessons, given low pass rates in the school. How might the whole class have benefitted if they had all been taught in terms which this boy could follow? How embarrassed was he about his very obviously 'special' treatment?

Still somewhat confused, the interviewer asked if the deputy head could 'sum up the policy of the school briefly' and he replied that he could not, adding: 'My concept of what the school is about is to focus on the learning cycle and to actually almost, as it were, prove to children that they can learn.' This 'language and communication' school's printed ENTRANCE CRITERIA listed 'needs' which ranged from 'an emphasis on social interaction skills to enable appropriate peer relationships to be formed' and 'differentiated material to provide access to the full national curriculum with additional emphasis on each childs [sic] particular strengths', to 'access to and constant use of computers' and 'the opportunity to participate in externally accredited exams'. These criteria could describe any student and be provided better in mainstream schools.

A science lesson

The science lesson with year 11 in the 'language and communication' school is devoted to one question written on the white board: 'A JCB uses 50,000 joules of energy to lift 8 tonnes of earth 5 metres. How efficient is it?' The teacher tries to get the class to suggest methods, but they cannot do so. Eventually he explains: 'Work done = 40,000 joules (tonnes times metres), energy = 50,000 joules. What is the percentage? Do it on your calculators.'

The walls of the science room are bare except for bits of sellotape, equipment is kept in a few shoe boxes. The lab bench doubles as a carpentry work bench with a vice on one side, and cuts and holes in the surface. 'You will be writing on paper and you must not use a surface with lots of holes in it,' repeats the teacher, but everyone stays sitting round the rough–hewn bench.

The classroom assistant tells the researcher that she 'does science' rather than following a class around. When asked if she is a lab technician she replies, 'Well not really, this lab is too small. I just tidy up.' Apart from fetching and later collecting up the calculators she sits watching the lesson.

The teacher walks up and down, from the board to the nearest boy whom he touches each time he is near him, holding his arm, patting his head, touching his hand many times over. No visual aids or teaching materials are used. When the teacher discusses four–fifths and eighty percent, no one appears to understand. The teacher and assistant spend nine minutes fetching the calculators from another room and giving them out to the six pupils. One boy asks for a different coloured one; he and the teacher argue, as if each wants to show who can exert most control, take up most time, and score most semi–joking points against the other. For the rest of the lesson, the teacher works through the problem orally with the whole class. They are unable to answer his questions. The calculators are not used. The assistant seems to be unfamiliar with them, because she tells the pupils to put the covers back on, without realising that these are already slotted on.

Ironically, the science lesson is symbolised by its topic, measuring a JCB's activity by the energy invested in it and the output it returned, with some allowance for 'inefficiency' in extra use of fuel to cope with friction. The mechanical concepts echo the language about pupils' 'linguistic input and appropriate output.' Much energy is wasted by friction, leading to extremely inefficient use of resources.

Art and music
In the junior 'language and communication' school, eight children in class 5–6 each have a flowerpot made from coiled clay. The pots are so alike that it seems impossible that the children had much share in making them. They now paint them inside and out. The assistant mixes powder paint to a uniform (not flecked) colour while they wait. At last palettes of paint are handed round. The assistant helps several children to ensure that the whole pot is painted. Carly talks to me enthusiastically about pets, and holds her brush at an angle which cannot reach inside her pot, but seems unaware of the problem. Concerned that she will be in trouble for not painting her pot, surreptitiously I move her arm to paint the pot while she talks. When they finish, the children move around rather aimlessly except for Jacob who rushes to the computer and dexterously sets up and plays with games which the teachers do not know how to set up. He is wearing adult–size trousers cut down to fit him and has holes in his jumper. He is so bright and active that he challenges the selection methods which allotted him to this school.

The next afternoon this class joins the younger year 3–4 class, giving one teacher free time. They watch a video about tapping out names and animal sounds on drums. Then they slowly line up and move into the next room, and sit round infant–sized tables with a big trolley of very good percussion instruments. One drum is sent round the table. After much sitting around, fidgeting, reprimanding and punishing, two drums are circulated. The children are supposed to beat their names simultaneously when a teacher lowers her raised arm, so they have to look at her, and the instrument, and respond to split second timing since she gives no warning about when she will move her arm, such as by counting a rhythm. There are chaotic ugly noises and much boredom among the fourteen waiting ones. Then food rhythms, fish and chips, and so on are ordered by the teacher. There is no piano or melodic instrument.

Some boys beat the drums violently, bang them as if they want to smash them out of impatience at waiting so long. A teacher stands behind one boy and holds his arm and beats the drum with his arm. The boy keeps wriggling and trying to move his arm away, shifting in his chair to get away from the teacher's body pressing over him.

Then a tape of Evelyn Glennie playing a complicated percussion ragtime is put on and everyone has an instrument which they bang or crash. As they have not yet had a chance to let off steam before they can start playing in different ways, such as softly, they crash all through Evelyn Glennie losing any rhythm. A tape of brass or steel bands, orchestras or choral music would provide a better background for them. The teacher and assistant keep yelling at them for being so loud. There is no pleasure in sound, rhythm, melody, vibrant or dramatic movement.

These lessons have been described to suggest that in the special schools we observed there can be vagueness in the remit, and a general uncertainty leads to and allows ineffective teaching. It could be argued that this creates learning difficulties instead of resolving them. We cannot be certain that the special schools we observed were not typical in this respect.

George

George shows how children can be just as much 'on trial' in a special school as they might be in a potentially excluding mainstream school. It may not be easy to find the appropriate school, and the quest can involve much disruption and insecurity. George started at an SLD nursery and then was moved to an assessment unit. His parents criticised the staff's lack of teaching and assessment skills, and believed that he was punished for behaviour related to his then unrecognized epilepsy with 'a lot of standing in corners'. The unit was part of an MLD school and eventually George's teacher decided that he could not cope and needed to return to the SLD school. The head teacher, however, resisted their 'fight' to move him, though by then they had enlisted a doctor. George's mother, Ann, said, 'I had someone they call as having a professional standing, it's not just a neurotic mother.' George's father, Hugh, added: 'He was in an awkward position, because he had to keep his numbers up or the school would have been closed.' Eventually George returned to the SLD school.

Ann: His nursery teacher was flabbergasted when she first saw us back at the school, as if she was saying, 'What on earth are you doing sending this child back here? He doesn't need it.'

Int: Do you wish he'd always stayed there and kept his friends and security?

Ann: Yes, yes. I don't think educationalists even give it a thought about children's feelings. It's just, 'Oh, we'll put them here or there.' Because you're just an inexperienced parent, you tend to listen to the advice you're given, and you don't yourself think well what's it doing for your child?

Hugh: We didn't really know what the situation was when children can speak less for themselves. It can be harder to parents to listen to them and speak for them or consider doing so.

When a child is not doing well at a school, parents trying to get more resources may enlist professionals who at times increase pessimism about the child's potential. George's parents involved an education psychologist who decided that George's speech was deceptively fluent.

Ann: He took him off in the kitchen and did all various assessments with him and I really liked him. He came back to us and said his speech is what is getting everybody. Do you realise there is nothing underneath? I was a bit shocked to have it confirmed, but –

Int: Nothing underneath?

Ann: He couldn't read. I said 'yes'. He can't read or write, his actual IQ was not particularly good, but his speech –

Hugh: He communicates very well indeed, very well indeed.

Int: With meaning and sense?

Hugh: He does make sense.

Ann: He does babble but he does also make sense.

Hugh: It's improved too, and this is why I'm cross about speech therapy not being adequate.

Ann: He likes to make up lots of stories.

Tensions between the parents' own views of George's abilities and their confidence in the psychologist's views were complicated by the context of their 'battle' to move George back to an SLD school. They needed to emphasise George's inability. It is questionable how much a negative assessment, based on very brief encounters and taking little account of the child's daily life, helps either the child or the parents. Even when—as is not always the case—assessors may accept that the child can have partly unknown potential and changing capacities, the assessments can be over-interpreted by others and become self-fulfilling prophecies.

In the listed building which his parents lease, the ebullient and articulate George talked for two hours. By contrast we encountered Vishal—also originally at an SLD school but now in a mainstream class at a relatively high-achieving East City comprehensive—who only uses one or two words at a time, and Ben (also at a comprehensive) whose difficulties are no less than George's. Yet George's parents insist that inclusion is appropriate for MLD but not for SLD, which they say George definitely is.

George does indeed 'make sense'. He is highly aware of his own performance within the (taped) interview: 'Oh mum, please, can I...ssssh!—sorry about that, ladies gentlemen'; 'can I go on about Rusty, my dog?'; 'pretend I'm on local radio'. He speaks at length about his parents' role as governors at his school ('Yes, I'm George Robbins from Dale End School, and yes, my mum's the chairman of the board of governors and, er, and my dad does the budget and he, er, he's another governor'), and complains that his father gets the budget wrong. He discusses local hospital closures and raises the possibility of taking the Department of Health to court over them or, alternatively, murdering the Secretary of State. He points out the absurdity of having his photo on the family car's disabled sticker in view of the fact that his father is just recovering from a major heart attack: 'why's it got my photo on there? why not his?' (George looks healthy and energetic).

He lists all his dislikes, introducing each with an accurate rendering of the Richard Wilson phrase 'I don't belieeeve...' The list includes his medication, the family's moving house, and his school: 'I want Dale End school to close down, I want all the staff to go bankrupt'; asked where he would like to go he names the school he previously attended, although this too is a 'special school, handicapped school, like Dale End—boring school.'

George discusses family history ('My grandfather worked in aerospace, yes, he was in Battle of Britain and he fly a harrier in 1922 and he park his harrier in the garden') and the possibility of his inheriting the house ('I really want to buy the lease...to look after it properly'). His mother's comment at this point is, 'Amazing what he picks up—you're talking and you find he has picked it up'; she acknowledges yet dismisses his abilities in one phrase, illustrating the tension in parental attitudes we referred to above. As for 'babble', it is true we have selected short phrases from George's interview; a longer transcript would reveal that his syntax is sometimes disconnected and the topics jump about. Nevertheless, it closely resembles the stream–of–consciousness writing of some twentieth–century novelists; much of this flow goes through most people's minds but they seldom say it all.

In addition, George seems very keen to take advantage of the unusual chance to offer his own opinions at length. If our perception is correct, then it is one example of how 'learning difficulties' may not just be inherent in an individual, as they are in every one of us, but are the consequences of an interaction between individual and context (Hart 1996): a notion that becomes much clearer when we look at children with learning difficulties who are in mainstream classes in ordinary schools.

Vishal: Down's syndrome in mainstream school

In Vishal's terraced house nine people from three generations live. Vishal is fourteen. He started at an SLD school but transferred to an ordinary school when he was eight, and is now in one of East City's mainstream comprehensives. His parents are elderly, and his mother's epilepsy has since led to mental illness. Vishal's two older brothers live in the house; responsibility for him and his parents has been taken on by the eldest brother, Kevel, and his wife, who have three young children of their own. Kevel works as an electrician. The bond between Vishal and Kevel is close. Kevel gives instructions to Vishal during the interview and is proud of him; at the same time Vishal's manner and personality clearly influence the relationship. Before the interview starts I am sitting alone with Vishal and I get him to help me set up my tape–recorder. I ask him if there's a socket, and he doesn't answer; so I hold up the plug and he immediately points to a socket in the wall behind me. The interview, which Vishal spontaneously interrupts in the middle of my first sentence to ask if I want tea, takes place in the kitchen. Kevel's own little children wander in occasionally, and Vishal sits them on his lap and cuddles them. At one point he comes over from his chair on the opposite side of the table and, pointedly removing the formal physical structure of a face–to–face interview, sits next to me on the settee. When I ask him who his friends are at school, he answers by listing nearly everyone in his class. At the time of interviewing, all East City primary–age children with Down's syndrome were starting in mainstream schools. Vishal, however, had started in an SLD school before the inclusion policy began. His brother had enquired about mainstream provision, but 'everything was just a dead end, we weren't even going to try for it;' even the social services day nursery had decided it could not cope with Vishal after one week. However, the change of culture created by the policy led to his SLD school itself initiating his transfer to mainstream.

> Kevel: Vishal was taken on at [local primary] school for a day a week to start with, then they thought he was doing quite well, and he started two days a week, and then they increased it to three days, and he eventually ended up going there full–time ... The teachers were quite good.

Normality and disability

At Vishal's comprehensive they are 'quite helpful'. Kevel's tone of voice is matter–of–fact, even diffident. This is characteristic of a number of East City parents we spoke to when asked to describe a time of change and possible anxiety. The families' concept of normality tends to be at variance with medical and educational concepts of disability. Doctors see mainly the child's pathology, and educational notions of 'special needs' and special expertise endorse this approach. Characteristically, families are said to be shocked when they first know of the diagnosis, and to come to 'accept' the pathology over time (Bicknell, 1988). Some researchers have assumed that when families speak about the normality of life with a disabled member, they are merely 'presenting' as normal (Voysey, 1975) what is self–evidently abnormal, to cover their anxiety. Yet this assumption seems to be loftily untrusting of ordinary people. Close research with families shows that often their notions of normality expand to incorporate the child with a disability (Goodey, 1998). They consequently expect that institutions beyond the family, such as schools, will share their wider view and experience of normality; the anxiety occurs when this does not take place. And so inclusion, if it occurs without a battle as is usually the case in East City, tends to be spoken about not as a triumph but simply as the child's due. When questioned about their views on inclusion as a general principle, Ben's parents appeared not to want to respond, and after two or three rephrasings of the question would only say 'Well it's about time this council did something right.'

However, Kevel is aware of the underlying ethical nature of the issue, and that it may be debated. In order to underline his beliefs about what is right for Vishal, he cites the fact that his disabled mother is also cared for at home; she sits on the stairs for the whole time I am there, staring ahead, and does not acknowledge anyone's presence. He is also clear about this in his attitude to other children:

> Everybody should be given the right to learn in mainstream ... At least that would make the other people and children aware of what other people go through in life ... If they see it with their own eyes, they can sort of understand or have a feeling about other people, you know, and that's another good thing—the other children learn from this,...looking at kids in their own class who are disabled and going through the same things as what they're doing, difficulties of their own. It's an education for the other kids.

Only once he has set out this ethical context does Kevel begin to talk about Vishal's behaviour and academic learning; the improvements in this respect seem (as to several other parents in East City) to be simply an offshoot rather than the point of inclusion. The SLD school was unsatisfactory because:

> What Vishal was doing was, you know, not what we were expecting ... With all due respect, Vishal was not, I mean he's a Down's syndrome but he's not really disabled in any other form ... In a way we were expecting that Vishal could do more ... He watches what other kids do. Before, you know, like he used to do what other kids do at Hope Valley [SLD school] but now you know like going to mainstream school he watches other kids and most of the time they're all sitting down in the class and he sits down and does his work. Like when he was at Hope Valley he used to come and just lay down on the floor and start rolling over 'cos he'd seen other kids doing it, so there's been quite a bit of improvement: behaviour, talking, education generally.

Vishal speaks to the interviewer in English mainly in single words, although in Gujarati he is a little more fluent. He tells me his favourite lessons and favourite sports. His desire to communicate is evident when it is obvious that I have not grasped what he is trying to say; he repeats it louder and more insistently until I understand. At his brother's prompting he shows me his school exercise books, which are neatly kept with very clear handwriting, and some paintings.

Both the actual situation of Vishal and Vishal's mother in the family and the tone of voice used by Kevel to describe it illustrate the concept of expanded normality described above. Classifications of pathological and normal, of 'moderate' and 'severe', seem in this context to be highly unstable. In Matthew's and George's schools the relationship between the individual and the (segregated) school context appears to increase their difference and difficulty.

Tracey and 'backwardness'

Children with learning difficulties in West County were constantly represented as abnormal—in their school, in transport to school, in the way most teachers referred to them, and in their general exclusion. The researcher interviewed one girl whose mother had attended the same special school and, seeing them later out shopping, realised with a sense of shock that in this setting her mother who looked so ordinary had, as a child, been marked out as entirely different. It is easier to classify and stigmatise children than adults into entirely different categories, and the main systems for doing this are the education and health services, which are intended for learning and healing.

In contrast, it could be argued that girls and boys with learning difficulties are a normal part of the warp and weft of family and neighbourhood life in East City. Before an interview with her parents, Tracey—who had at one time been in an SLD school—was chatting with a group of women on the pavement outside her house, and later took a full part in the discussion. In the following extract, during which a neighbour walked in through the open door from the road outside, the tone of Tracey's mother's remark 'I'm being interviewed' clearly denotes considerable pride rather than any awkwardness attached to Tracey's disability.

> Maureen (mother): Oh hello Shal, come in—I'm being interviewed. Right, what do you want, mate?
>
> Sharon: Only just to tell you they got no more of those dresses, but I've got a black one, and...
>
> Dave (father): Really?
>
> Sharon: Yes dear, but not that type.
>
> Dave: Ain't one of them lacy numbers, is it?
>
> Tracey: Shal, we been round the pub again lunchtime.
>
> Maureen (to Dave): Oh? Who did you go with?
>
> Dave (sheepish mumble): Brian and that.
>
> Maureen: Oh. Yeah go on.
>
> Sharon: And it buttons all the way down the front...
>
> Dave: Nice./
>
> Sharon: /and it's got straps which tie up round the back/
>
> Dave: Leather boots?
>
> Tracey: You'll never wear it mum!
>
> Maureen: I will.

Tracey: I'll have it!
Dave: Bring it round and model it, give us a twirl and everything.
Sharon: What's the matter with him? Who's been winding him up?
Maureen: I don't know—he's been on night work, ain't he.
Sharon: Right, see you later. Bye.
Maureen: Bye. [To researcher] Yeah, I was going to say ...

Tracey started in a mainstream infants' class before East City's inclusion policy had begun, and encountered problems. Her parents describe them:

Maureen: The policy was, like, all right we'll take her in, but she either fits in with us or ... That Mrs Browning [headteacher], I'll tell you, she was very patronising. From round [the primary] school. Very—wasn't it—'Oh it must be sooo hard for you' [change from cockney to a Lady Bountiful accent], and I used to think 'shut up', know what I mean? ... I've got five children altogether, and she's no different from any of the other four. Yeah. I want release from my other children as well—drive me crackers.
Dave: That Mrs Browning, now you can't put your point across because she don't know where you're coming from.

In spite of her parents' insistence, Tracey was taken out of her infants' school and placed in an SLD school:

Maureen: I said we ain't having her there.
Dave: And we said no, 'cos see we knew for a fact that she was all right, she was backward in respect that she was/
Maureen: /so many years behind/
Dave: /so many years behind, but/
Maureen: there wasn't nothing wrong with her/
Dave: /they was trying to put forward that she was backward *backward.* You know? And that's where they wanted to shut the door, all they wanted to do was just say well she's a backward child, end of.

Four years later, aware only that she 'was really really fed up,' Maureen

went to the education office and said, 'I want Tracey in a mainstream school.' So she [officer] said, 'Well put her in there, then—you could have had her back at [the local mainstream school] at any time,' so I said, 'Well why didn't nobody tell me?' You see, nobody gives this information.

Tracey spent her last primary year in the mainstream school which had rejected her four years earlier. Change in the overall LEA policy and a change in headteacher—an overall change in culture—ensured that the school was now 'all right'. She then went to the local comprehensive where we observed her.

The parents' comments on 'backwardness' raise the question of assessment. Much of the literature criticising the usefulness of IQ and mental age scores asserts that 'intelligence' is not biologically determined or hereditary, but shaped by life–chances and environment (Gould, 1984). This is then used to argue against attributing low intelligence in a stereotypical way to certain groups of people: such scores, it is said, are relative and depend on environmental factors. But this argument is invariably assumed to be about the 'normal' population, and the underlying assumption may still remain that IQ and mental age scores are a useful way of looking at someone with an acknowledged learning difficulty.

The parents' criticism here questions the relevance and usefulness the 'mental age' score entirely. Historically, the role of such scores and of the educational psychologist was administrative, determining separate placement according to the number of separate places available in a particular area. Over the years the emphasis has shifted towards using global scores as quasi–medical evidence that children ought, by virtue of their individual difficulties, to be in one kind of school rather than another. The inclusive setting of East City leads to different insights into the system. One educational psychologist, Katherine, told us how she regretted the way in which the psychological advice attached to a statement becomes

> an end in itself ... It's almost like a child should have a coat, a hat, a pair of gloves, a statement ... It's a psychology thing, you know, once that's a table, once I see that as a table, there is no way I can think of it as a chair, even if everybody in your family, visitors to the house what have you, sits on it ... That's what labels do. The IQ test has never been useful for anyone, it's only been used to prove people's arguments against things.

An individual learning programme

When Tracey first arrived at her secondary comprehensive, after only six months in a mainstream primary, she went round taking hold of teachers' hands. The head described to us how she wasn't sure whether responding would mean encouraging her, but described this as a learning experience for herself: allowing for differences of behaviour among pupils with learning difficulties gradually led to the school being less rigid in its behaviour codes.

Within the range of GCSE options for years 10 and 11 there is an 'individual learning programme' designed for pupils labelled as having special needs. Much of the time they bring work from other lessons; this helps to avoid their being withdrawn for extra help during those lessons. (There is mixed ability teaching throughout the school, with the exception of GCSE maths). Two students with considerable learning difficulties have not chosen the individual learning programme as an option. However, two non–statemented pupils have chosen it because it is quiet and allows more time for their other work; one boy was working on a Sylvia Plath poem.

There are eight boys in the room and Tracey. The atmosphere is calm and purposeful. Tracey is extremely observant about things others tend to forget. This is sometimes helpful. A boy comes in halfway and the class teacher immediately sorts out some work for him. 'He needs a late slip, miss.' 'Good point, Tracey,' says the class teacher, and she would obviously have forgotten if not reminded. Tracey is working on the computer. Neither she nor I can work the cursor. The instant she sees I can't do it, she doesn't wait for me but calls out 'Miss!' (Miss is intently involved with another pupil). I feel I ought to have a strategy for preventing her uninhibited interruptions of all the other adults to ask for a disc, to make it work, and make the cursor work. Tracey has been asked to compose riddles. She tries to write a bit, then dictates to me 'It is a fruit, it is yellow', etc. She copies my writing, typing very quickly on a keyboard. She is triumphant when I (genuinely) don't get 'banana' in spite of having three guesses including, pathetically, 'orange' and 'a yellow apple'.

A science lesson
Tracey tells me she likes science because they teach you how to burn things, so I go with her to her science lesson. We do bar–graphs about the height of pea plants. The lesson consists entirely of sitting at desks drawing. I recall another lesson on the same topic I once observed, in which Mendel's theory of genetics was illustrated by lining the pupils up and pointing out differences in height, eye colour etc. Although on the one hand the lesson is fairly uninspiring and pupils respond with considerable extraneous chatter, the teacher is nevertheless aware of the need to differentiate the lesson so that the work which Tracey does matches her abilities at that stage. A classroom assistant accompanies Tracey to some lessons, including this one. She asks me, 'Are you going to be joining in or just observing? Tracey's a bit high because she's seen you in here. Otherwise she'll manipulate the situation.' I decide to observe. Tracey is working on a table with four other girls and the assistant, who is

working with all of them. This group is working very hard, unlike the others who are noisy. The subject teacher says it's a rather disruptive class. Some work is getting done in spite of this.

The subject teacher comes over to me several times. She tells me that she is trying to deal with two boys who won't work with Tracey. However, the teacher says that when the assistant is not there other pupils step unasked into her role; she adds, 'I think that's nice.' I ask her how she fits Tracey into a class which is studying for GCSE; her judgement is that 'She can learn some science. In this lesson, for example, she can learn that she looks like her parents as do other people, that some characteristics look like one parent or the other or even her grandparents. She can share learning with the others, however basic the terms.' The teacher says 'it's a shame' that the rigid examination system means they will not enter Tracey, since the teacher assessment is that she will not obtain a grade.

This example shows that inclusion does not necessarily depend on inspired teaching, a perfectly behaved student group or on extra special expertise, even in mainstream schools. This teacher's need to think about Tracey's individual abilities and difficulties with the science curriculum may stimulate her to think more clearly about the abilities and difficulties of all the other students and gradually increase her own teaching skills.

An inclusive primary school

Seymour accepts all local children whatever their ability. It is also resourced to take disabled children who live further away and everyone benefits from the higher staffing ratio they bring with them. Among the statemented children on the roll of 450 were 32 with severe learning difficulties, some of whom had profound and multiple difficulties. People from many ethnic groups live in the area, including refugees and asylum–seekers. The school does not have a uniform because some children cannot wear one, and among the many variedly dressed people most of the disabled children mix unnoticed. All the staff, including supply teachers and students, are helped to ensure continuity by notices in every classroom with reminders about attending to each child's equal physical access to all the people and resources in the room, and mental access to rich opportunities for learning and relating. 'Does each child have equal time? ... Are staff fully deployed and aware of their roles? Is a mixture of children involved in activity—gender, race and need? Is group work co–operative? Are you supportive of each child's initiatives?' As mentioned earlier, the staff encourage relationships between many children, rather than reinforcing the exclusive pairs and small groups which children form in most schools.

Seymour is well resourced, and that is because special schools in East City have been closed and the funds diverted into mainstream. A huge range of equipment is used in almost every session. The only way this can be managed is for everyone to share in keeping the rooms tidy, and the books and materials in good condition. They all, except the most disabled children, clear up after each task and prepare the room for the next session so that everyone can then start work immediately. Some children arrive at 8am or stay on after school, and they can go into the classrooms to help the staff. All shelves and drawers are labelled with words and pictures of the equipment they hold. Notices on access have reminders to place everything at a level every child can reach. Cleaning up tasks, from 'make sure pen lids are back on and worn–out pens discarded' to 'mop the toilet', are listed on wall notices, which say:

At the end of each session is everyone equally involved in tidying up?
Do they know the expectations?
Is it fast?
Are instructions clear?
Is equipment complete and put away in the correct place?
Most of these activities can and should be done by or with children as part of taking responsibility for what they have done.

Staff learn from disabled students ways of improving the school which benefit everyone and save time. Instead of set break times, students take a morning break or go to PE as it fits in with their work, so there are no queues. Outside areas are staffed and equipped to enable everyone to work in or outside through the day.

Classes clear up before lunch and then sit in quiet reading or discussion groups. Messengers arrive every few minutes to call a few more children to the small, very crowded canteen. A short queue of children waits to collect their trays, choose from a varied menu, and then find a spare seat as earlier diners finish. They carry the trays carefully through the narrow spaces. The staff, who eat with the children, help the most disabled ones. An autistic boy with no speech and quite challenging behaviour picks up two handfuls of custard, and his helper smiles and cleans his hands; everyone else takes little notice. There are three orderly sittings, with very little overt adult supervision.

The head teacher's philosophy is summed up in the phrase, 'at this school, all staff teach all children.' The school has an open plan, with each wing devoted to a particular age–appropriate key stage. Children move about at will. All children have a diary for the day, in which they list the activities they intend to do and write comments about them afterwards; staff collate the diaries and enter records at the end of each day.

In the Key Stage 1 area is a little girl who seems to be having trouble writing the day and date at the top of her diary. Other children on the table tell me her name, and when we have finished they say to me 'Take her to the reading area, she wants to look at a book.' We go to the reading area and she gives me 'Good morning Franny', about a girl in a wheelchair. Another girl comes up and listens, holding a book, 'Old MacDonald', which she wants me to read to her next. None of this is supervised; it just seems to happen. We are suddenly interrupted by a large boy, about ten, who has come from the next–door area and noticed a new face. He has recently learned how to hold someone else's hands and clap them, and he wants to demonstrate it to me. He jumps up and down constantly. We play the game, while the girl waits patiently with Old MacDonald. I do the same to him, holding his arms while he claps his hands. He doesn't want to leave. A classroom assistant is standing nearby, and he keeps taking hold of my hands while she tries to persuade him to leave. But she doesn't pull him away or shout at him, or say very much; it is obviously up to me to turn away, so I do. We carry on with Old MacDonald. It suddenly occurs to me that I have been subconsciously hearing the loud groaning noise made by the big boy on and off since arriving, but since there are lots of other noises in the open–plan area—children talking in normal voices, banging in the woodwork corner—I haven't registered the groaning as odd. Then I spend some time playing with the sand. I talk to another boy who is playing there and he doesn't respond; I don't know whether he doesn't want to or whether he has some profound difficulty.

The difference between ordinary children and others doesn't seem obvious when they mix freely with each other, whereas segregation highlights difference. The intensive activity, range of resources, the highly organised teaching framework and demanding expectations create an atmosphere of normality which has expanded to include disabled children and in which everyone is busy; even those with profound and multiple difficulties are reported by parents to be more alert. In all these respects there is a contrast with the special schools for learning difficulties we observed.

In the Key Stage 2 area two boys are discussing how to grow plants and are tending baby sunflowers in pots. They tell me what they are doing in a naturally egalitarian manner that seems to pervade the classrooms. A girl comes over— I'm sitting between her and the bookcase—and asks directly, 'Can you get me that book please?' The boys have been learning about the second world war and ask me if I took part in it; another group ask me if I am their teacher's father. I meet two ten–year–old boys, Jaswinder and Dermot. Jaswinder asks me why I haven't got a beard; as I later learn from his class teacher, it is the only thing he ever says to an adult male. Dermot is cutting out large decorated letters spelling Jaswinder's name. Jaswinder has a pair of scissors too and is trying to cut the remnants. Dermot obviously thinks, or has been told, that Jaswinder shouldn't have the scissors and takes them away, but humanises his action by telling Jaswinder that it's no use cutting the waste. His tone of voice is serious and paternal but pleasant. The class teacher helps Jaswinder to sort the letters of his name in the right order, telling me afterwards that he performed well because a visitor was there. On the other hand, Dermot is very clearly not putting on a performance. For him Jaswinder is just there; the world contains people like Jaswinder, and when you're with them you just do what is sensible. The class teacher announces it's time for lunch and I see Dermot and Jaswinder's hands slip into each other, in a way which clearly happens often. Dermot is looking after Jaswinder, who would otherwise wander, but it seems to be a relationship as well as a duty.

The teacher in charge of the Key Stage 2 area tells me about a parent who came to see her, worried about her son's progress. She felt he was not doing as well as he should. The mother went on, 'It's because the disabled children are here, isn't it?' The teacher tells me how she felt that the moment she had been expecting for the last three years had finally arrived. Her first instinct was to remember advice about 'bringing people with you'; a defensive reply started to formulate itself in her mind, for example to say that the year 6 SATs results had improved in the year–group which had been the first to contain disabled pupils. She rejected this in favour of what she was about to say—that if they didn't like it they could take their son somewhere else—when the mother continued and said that it didn't matter because she wanted her son to be where there are disabled children because it was better for him.

Ben at Jacksons Lane Comprehensive

Like George, Ben has epilepsy; he fits several times a week and has associated learning difficulties. His room in a council flat has just enough space for a bed and one chair. His father has painted the walls, with a white band halfway up all round, and has stencilled an assortment of words which obviously refer to the things Ben likes (pizzas, nanny, music etc.). Ben tells me that he likes 'any pop stuff, like rock songs or things like Michael Jackson, Gary Glitter and all that,' and how he likes using the keyboard in school music lessons. Best of all,

> I do writing. I done it on the computer, I been writing in lots of books
> and I done it in science and that, I do the computers in a thing called

IT. Some things I get er...I have a few problems with like capital letters and my full stops. Where I should put capital letters I give up ...

Ben describes to me the kind of support he gets in the classroom:

Int: Do you do science with everybody else, or in a small group?
Ben: Do it with the class, but I mean I'm not by myself, I'm not put by myself, I have a carer with me, Marilyn.
Int: Does she help you, Marilyn?
Ben: Yeah. She, like, if I can't see the writing from the blackboard she has like a little writing book and she writes it for me down in that. And I copy it from there.
Int: Does she help anybody else?
Ben: Yeah. Like if they get stuck or anything she just goes round the school and helps the kid, goes round the class and helps the children that don't know what to do.

Ben interrupts a conversation about his dislike of Religious Education to start talking about his relationships in class:

Ben: Halfway through the lesson I'm trying to fight myself to get my bag back...'cos one of the kids, this kid's a bully and he's a very selfish boy. He goes punching me sometimes, and then once in history—he's in my history class as well—I put my bag down somewhere and I was on my way taking my coat off to get ready for the lesson, and then he just picked my bag up and took it over to his table ... And then all I have to do is tell a teacher and he gives it back to me. That's all I do, I wouldn't touch him or nothing, otherwise I'd just get myself into trouble ... And if it goes on he has to stay in late or something like that, doing lines, like 'I must not take somebody else's equipment that doesn't even belong to me', and write it out about ten times.
Int: Who are your mates?
Ben: I've got one in there called Richard Greaves, another one called Abdul Ibrahim, he's in a wheelchair, and I've got some others about as well.
Int: Who are the others?
Ben: I've got one called Hakim, and another, a girl called Janice ... She's like big–built, she looks like she's about sixteen, and she's quite nice ... things like if my bag's hanging down from my arm while I'm carrying it and it's come off my shoulder she'll lift it back on again.
Int: Is she in your class?

Ben: No, I just see her every day when I go up to registration.

Ben tells me about the way his week is structured, and his feelings about
the difference between the main school and the resource area. As with his
comments about Marilyn, the classroom assistant, they show that he is fully
aware of his position within the school as someone with recognized learning
difficulties:

Int: So when you go to these lessons, are you in a big class or a small
       class?
Ben: In a big class, I think there's about sixty.
Int: That's quite a lot.
Ben: I do go to different classes, though, like the kids that's in the same
       registration class as me, I still go to that class. And sometimes they're
       in some lessons with me, like English and maths and art and music,
       and science, but there's like the resource area and the main school, and
       I go to French in the resource area on a Thursday and I do living skills
       there on a Friday.
Int: So do you like being in the resource area or do you like being in the
       main school?
Ben: I like being in the resource area, I think I prefer it.
Int: Why is that?
Ben: Because sometimes like in the main school, if you've just started a
       piece of writing you've got to hurry up and finish it within ten minutes,
       and plus listening to the teacher—sometimes I can't manage it.
Int: So how much time do you spend in the resource area?
Ben: Just on Thursday when I have French lessons, and Friday living
       skills, the rest of the time I'm in the main school.

I thank Ben for talking to me and explain once again why I am doing the
interviews, then he takes me downstairs to sit with his mother and father round
a small table in their kitchen. The baby brother spends most of his time asleep
on his father's lap, while Ben disappears to do something else. They corroborate
some of the things Ben has said. I ask if Brenda and Jimmy, Ben's parents,
feel that Ben is too tied to the classroom assistant:

Brenda: No, but Ben looks at it: the carer's only there to write the things
          down that he hasn't got time for, or to be there in case he has a fit. And
          that's all she's there for, you know, so he doesn't mind being with that

person all day, so that's pretty good, you know. He's pretty friendly with all the teachers, and he don't mind any of them.

Jimmy talks about the friend Janice, and as we observed in other schools a close relationship can grow between children with physical disabilities or learning difficulties and those whose behaviour is a problem in school:

> Well, so far from what I've seen of round there, they're very good. I mean, the kids you'd think there would be problems with, like the older kids—considering the area and that—but it's often the roughest ones who are most protective. Yeah, there's a little crowd of them round there, these girls, what you'd call them hard nuts, I think they had to expel one of the girls there for carrying a knife, but you look at this Janice and see her with Ben it's like a different person, she keeps an eye on him, like—not, she don't smother him or anything, it's just like she sees he's all right every now and then.

Zoe's mother had spoken to us about her daughter in the same school, who has severe learning difficulties and sometimes becomes aggressive. A member of staff with some responsibility for her, and who according to her parents was opposed to having her in the school, had been punishing Zoe by the school's uniform behaviour code. This led to several temporary exclusions and an exacerbation of the original problem. The head teacher's approach to the behaviour code was changed partly as a result of the way Zoe was protected by a self-appointed group in her class. They reported to the parents whenever any of these incidents occurred and thus enabled them to discuss with staff alternative methods of dealing with the problem.

'The same but slightly different'

Ben's parents compare his mainstream primary school with the comprehensive:

> Brenda: I think Napier [primary], although they take the kids and try and make them feel part of the school and not feel different, they don't realise the problems that puts on the children. The children are ill, but they're told you can do this and you can do that, you know, they're trying to make them—for want of a better way of saying it—normal—and you can't. I can't make Ben normal. It puts more pressure on the children, I think so, to try and make them normal is wrong; you tell them they're special, they're different, you don't know why but they are, and as long as the kids know they're going to be accepted that way, it goes.

Jimmy: The problem with Napier is, they didn't understand the problems
or the needs of these children what had got these problems, they hadn't
got the experienced teachers there. They had a good attitude but they
was too laid back. Inexperience, really. But then having said that, them
kids up at Napier have grown up with him, and to them fits are normal.
And why shouldn't they? I mean when you look around, most kids
most probably have grown up with someone in their family or close to
them, whatever, where there's a disability of some kind.
Brenda: Yeah, yeah, yeah. I mean there again he might have gone to
another school where they didn't have the knowledge or whatever, but
they might have thought that Ben was some sort of freak. They just
don't know how to handle them the same but slightly different. I mean
they are different to a certain extent, but no matter what's wrong with
a kid, whether they can't walk, whether they have fits or whatever,
they're still human, they've still got feelings.

Our experience of Napier was indeed that it was a school which was
determined to enact East City's inclusion policy by taking all catchment area
children, but which interpreted inclusion—initially at least—as the avoidance
of outside help if at all possible. Napier had to learn to treat them 'the same
but slightly different.' Expecting optimistically that any child can be made to
fit a 'normal' environment, or pessimistically pathologising them from the
outset, are both approaches which are too simplistic to accommodate difference.

Introducing inclusion: does practice or principle come first?

Ben's parents amicably disagree about local policy during the interview. Brenda
is more critical. She attended a special school herself for two years, and has
high expectations of what an inclusion policy should mean in practice;
essentially, everything should be in place before it starts. Her husband argues
that this is impractical; people should do what they can, if the principle is
important, and see from there how to move it forwards. Can inclusion only be
done if the right attitudes and resources are in place before anything starts?
Again, the debate between them reflects the real world of inclusion politics. It
hinges on the cookery room. Jackson's Lane is an old set of buildings which
was given lifts and mobility access throughout when East City's physically
disabled school closed, so that it could take a proportion of those children.
However, the cookers were a normal height, unsuitable for wheelchair users,
and had not been changed:

Jimmy: The more people are wised up on [inclusion], eventually, as these
kids get older and run their own businesses like some of them, they go

bloody hell, they got [to get] a ramp in here—you got to educate other people, it's like educating the education department/

Brenda: /I don't know, 'cos Ben said...kids in wheelchairs can't use the ovens, they're too high—so if they're going to do it/

Jimmy: /that's what I'm saying, they've only just mixed them [students], it's only been going for a year.

Brenda: They've got to do it properly, not half do it, not just put a lift and a ramp in and say the wheelchairs can just get up and that's it. They got to do more, because/

Jimmy: /that's the trouble, ain't it, they've only just integrated them.

Brenda: Yeah, but if we don't speak up...[and] they must be saving money 'cos they're shutting them [special schools] all down.

Jimmy: I mean the teachers must come across that problem every day of the week, I mean you've got the cookery teacher there, she must be saying to the headmaster 'Look, how can I teach the kids when the cookers are too high for them?' and he'll probably say 'Well we've spent all the money we can, for this year, we've put the lifts and ramps in, we've altered the playing field...' but then they got no more money left and now they got to wait till next year when they can do it. I mean their hands are tied as much as what ours are. It's no good shouting at the teachers in the school, you got to shout at the department.

Brenda: Well, you shout at the department and you tell them you don't try and do it till you can afford it.

Jimmy: But then you'll never do it. If we didn't go doing what we're doing now, we'd be going backwards—no one would ever learn.

Brenda: Yeah, they have got to mix, I'm not saying they haven't.

Jimmy: We'd end up having centres again, where all the disabled kids are in there making wicker baskets.

Brenda: But if they're gonna build it, they got to build it right. It's no good half doing it...

Jimmy: And the only way they can do it is by closing the [special schools] down.

Brenda: If you got a car out there and it's got no engine in it, it's no good to you—you can't use it. So if you've got a school building without all the facilities for the special needs, it's not going to work.

Jimmy: That's the thing though, ain't it, it's got to be trial and error ... this was the first time it's ever been done, I suppose, and they've gone like, well let's put them all in together for now instead of integrating them slowly or however everybody would have liked it to be done. It's

been done now, that's a stage, and next time they do it...they'll most
probably have a different way of doing it.

From the standpoint of people who are experiencing an inclusion policy
which is matched with the closure of the special schools, the familiar canon
that inclusion is a process, not a state, means something very concrete, and
gives them a perspective which looks to future possibilities:

Jimmy: Like what you were saying, the cooker level, it's some of the
         things have just been overlooked and needs moving on. I mean you
         could point some of them out, couldn't you, and say 'you've forgotten
         about that side' ... What you don't want to happen is, five years down
         the line, it's become complacent. You know, kids just being put in the
         classroom and/
Brenda: No, they got to improve it, not just leave it/
Jimmy: Like now, they're all up on it, all the teachers are wised up, but
         then in four to five years you get 'Oh, we know it all,' you get settled
         into a way of life...rather than someone going round saying, 'I think
         things are falling down a little bit here.' I think they should have an
         independent person or body just goes around and keeps everybody on
         their toes a little bit.

Much of the extensive literature on integration and inclusion implies that
these are esoteric, expert matters. Here we show ordinary people summing up
the key points of the debate and illustrating how in the end it is not an expert
decision but one based on personal beliefs about human nature and philosophies
of political change. We discuss these in our conclusion.

Much of the extensive literature on integration and inclusion implies that
these are esoteric, expert matters. Here we show ordinary people summing up
the key points of the debate and illustrating how in the end it is not an expert
decision but one based on personal beliefs about human nature and philosophies
of political change. We discuss these in our conclusion.

Much of the extensive literature on integration and inclusion implies that
these are esoteric, expert matters. Here we show ordinary people summing up
the key points of the debate and illustrating how in the end it is not an expert
decision but one based on personal beliefs about human nature and philosophies
of political change. We discuss these in our conclusion.

Chapter 5

PHYSICAL AND SENSORY IMPAIRMENTS

*Linda: My [mainstream] school is a special school because I've made
lots of new friends there and I get lots of help with my work.*

This chapter reports strong contrasts between West County's and East City's
practices and attitudes towards students with physical and sensory impairments.

Special schools in West County

The two special day–boarding schools observed are each in a historic country
house some distance from a small village. Douglas Bader School for physically
impaired students is similar to the SLD school in its generally kind and gentle
staff and relaxed routines. The pupils manoeuvre wheelchairs skilfully, seeming
to take care not to hurt one another as if they know physical and emotional
pain too well. Originally with senior and sixteen–plus departments, the school
is building up a primary department, whose teacher feels ambivalent.

> I believe strongly in integration but I worry about what happens to the
> ones who apply here and cannot get in. We shouldn't be so isolated,
> miles from anywhere, we should be on a campus with mainstream
> schools. But children would lose out at mainstream, no physio, no
> therapists, no nurses. Yet the more able ones here are not working at
> the correct pace, though they're very happy to come and they're very
> unhappy in mainstream.

She arranges for her class of ten children aged nine to eleven to visit local
primary schools to present work at joint assemblies and conduct ceremonies
like giving out paper friendship rings. Videos of the visits show headmasters
welcoming the visitors: 'Today is a very special day and it is special because
you have come to see us.' The girls at the ordinary schools tend to play as
instructed with the disabled children, for example at acting circuses, while
most boys run around awkwardly avoiding them. The mission statement says
the school aims 'to provide a safe and secure environment, wide ranging
opportunities, quality education, care and therapy in order to promote happiness,
self–dependence, confidence and self–worth for children and young people
who have special needs aimed at enabling each of them to have these met and
to participate in and contribute to society in the way he or she chooses.'

Louis Braille School for visually impaired students has high SATs and GCSE results. The staff say their main aim is to provide the best possible academic education, and one as 'normal as possible' to enable students to overcome limitations, and to 'shine at what they are best at'. Louis Braille is very selective and seeks to be like a grammar school; thus there is selection within selection. The lessons observed often involved exceptionally good teaching by very knowledgeable and critically thoughtful staff. They skilfully encourage the students to work out their own questions, answers and imaginative responses, in small, usually orderly classes. During their interviews, blind boys and girls enthusiastically argue about politics and religion, history and philosophy, showing their expansive vision of the world. The only blind teacher is a member of the European Commission funded HELIOS (Handicapped Europeans Living in an Open Society). She regularly makes international visits, tests new equipment and inspects integration initiatives. The only partially sighted teacher also works abroad, in Asia, and it can feel odd to arrive at this isolated old building and encounter international perspectives and the newest technology. Run by a charity which generously supplements LEA placements, the site has purpose built primary and secondary blocks, a 16+ resource college and an expanding nursery. Nursery places are free and children who travel in long distances can start to board from five years. Classes go riding, play music, some students enter international swimming events and, during the weeks observed, all the primary school took part in a satirical, musical version of Cinderella.

Entry to special schools: selecting students

Teachers in both schools describe a changing clientele. Many of their potential pupils, including the most impaired ones, now attend mainstream schools. Special schools are left, increasingly, with students who may be less disabled but who, because they also have behavioural or learning difficulties, are less welcome in ordinary schools. Douglas Bader school was founded for students with average to high intellectual abilities. One teacher said:

> There used to be several grammar–type schools for physically handicapped children, but now I think there's only one left and the high fliers go there from all over the country, or they go to mainstream. Not many of our children take GCSEs now, and in a year or two no one will here. Some of them could do more GCSEs, but we can't put on a whole course just for two or three of them.

Some of the students say that being held back makes them doubly disabled, and getting the best possible qualifications is even more important for them if they are to compete for college places and careers. Some students at Douglas Bader walk unaided, some with crutches. It is now common for people using wheelchairs to attend mainstream schools, so Douglas Bader does not necessarily admit the most severely disabled ones. Those with profound and multiple learning difficulties like Stacy go to SLD schools in West County and to ordinary schools in East City; most Douglas Bader pupils are in a middle range of disability. One LEA officer said that Douglas Bader had been rapidly getting smaller, and so it increased the number of pupils who have more severe epilepsy, medical conditions or learning difficulties than it used to accept.

Louis Braille now has fewer blind students than partially sighted ones. Some can read large print and use magnifying aids, enabling them to use ordinary school materials. A growing literature offers practical guidelines for mainstream teachers, and reports successful integration of impaired students of all ages (Gross, 1993). One mother repeated points made by other parents:

> The blind children or braillies [braille users] like my son are disadvantaged by the partially sighted ones who could manage in ordinary schools with a few aids. They don't need special teachers, but they're disruptive and they make unfair demands on the teachers' time. And you don't any longer get the real experts who specialised in teaching blind children. You get teachers coming in straight from mainstream schools with no special skills at all. They can't even read braille and those who can mostly don't know enough to teach braille. They find it easier to teach the partially sighted children, and they like them because they help to get good results for the school and we do very well in the league tables. But if all the partially sighted children left, the school would not be viable. I suppose it would have to close... Some of the blind children at the school have brain tumours and are terminally ill. I know they've got to go somewhere but it's not fair on the ones like my son if they are at his kind of school. My son was severely bullied, and it is difficult when the other children can't see what is going on.

A teacher described Sammie, 'She can see quite well and she's really here because of family disruption. She wants to be like the others and she's taught herself braille. When we do art she insists on being like them and using German paper' (which retains impressions so that drawings can be felt). One of the older boys said; 'The problem is that this school has ended up with a lot of people with difficulties other than sight which the teachers can't handle.'

Another reason for the varying levels of disability in these special schools is that they absorb less disabled students from West County and nearby LEAs who, in areas without a special school, would attend mainstream schools. In so doing, the special schools also drain away expertise and the impetus towards integration from a wide surrounding area by advertising that they can provide better services. Special school staff tend to be convinced that the benefits of special schooling outweigh any problems. They frequently (perhaps not always intentionally) criticise mainstream schools:

> An adviser went with a mother to a meeting to persuade staff at her local school to accept her son, but the teachers were so hostile. The mother felt it was appalling, a terrible experience, and she said, 'I'd begun to convince myself he could take his place in society and now I don't think it is so.' She was so dreadfully shocked and hurt by their prejudice she decided that she would never let her son go to that school.

Some students hold similar views. Lesley uses a wheelchair, and described being taunted by bullies and forced into shoplifting by a protection racket at her former mainstream school. With several of her friends, she spoke with horror about cruel teasing and the loneliness for disabled students at mainstream schools. Their views may have been reinforced in that everyone at Lesley's school had either never attended mainstream or had left because, for some reason, they were not thought able to cope. Criticising these schools was one way of maintaining their self–respect. In West County (at least) criticism of other schools by pupils and adults was common, state versus private schools, high versus grammar, and mainstream versus special schools. Yet being at special school is not easy. Michelle, aged fifteen, spoke of feeling tormented by a care worker, and being depressed and suicidal at times, though she greatly enjoyed attending a mainstream Christian Easter camp.

Entry to the Douglas Bader and Louis Braille Schools is influenced by how families are informed, the resources and attitudes in their local schools, their beliefs about the best kinds of schooling, and varying advice from health and social services staff. These are social–political not physical–clinical factors. One LEA senior officer in West County summed up the strong pressures which support special schools:

> Lots of parents are got at by interest groups very early on, the language disordered, or autistic tendency or behaviour disorder, or whatever the label. These well meaning lobbyists are desperate to widen their group of children—almost anyone is autistic now, the same with aphasia and

dyslexia. And parents are very much influenced by someone saying, 'You get your child into a special school, that's the best place.' It's partly about being sold to a specialist, 'Your child isn't going to develop unless you've got a specially trained person.'

Then parents get extremely distressed because their child's problem isn't being treated and there are terrific behaviour problems, children failing, bullying—very sad cases. And many of these problems can be cleared up once appropriate teaching is provided without needing special referral. We've set up several facilities for visual impairment in mainstream schools and will continue to do so.

The child development centres do a tremendous job. The problem is they're health orientated, they have a senior medic responsible and they call in the teaching hospital and they like to label because they are medics.

A few special schools do incredible things in terms of advertising and undermining our integration policy. At one stage, they were developing out–reach for in–reach, you know, pull kids in. You've got to be on your guard all the time for people who don't want to see inclusion. I have hellish times with parents. Their meetings [at special schools] can be extremely draining, a bit like being nailed to a cross and I don't say that flippantly. Special schools are genuine in their belief that children are best served by special schools. They simply have a business and if the business goes down, they go down with it.

You've got to ask: it's all very well saying this mainstream placement isn't appropriate for this child, but what is a special school doing that is so wonderful and good? How do we know this child is going to be developing? One autism school didn't stand up to these questions and we've done a lot of work with them to change the school.

Louis Braille now supports more of its boarders in local mainstream and private schools by day and with special support for evening homework. Asked if this was outreach, the head teacher replied: 'Oh no, not at all. We are trying to avoid that. We see ourselves as providing support where we can do it best, games, geography with tactile maps and models, mobility and life skills work.' In some ways, these aids can encourage unusually realistic understanding. One boy said, 'When they show you a map, I can't imagine the world like that, all flat, I've got so used to the feeling glance.' The head teacher emphasised that aids are not enough, special teaching skills are essential. 'You can't be spontaneous, you must plan ahead to ensure you have the aids you need. If you are joking, you have to make this clear with them because they cannot see your face.' Other staff also emphasised the difference in being blind: 'On the masters' course we learnt that 80% of what normal children learn is through what they see.' 'The blind professor said that he stands on the kerb and hears the motorists sweep past him like gods.'

Yet these kinds of quotes are questionable. Few teachers are now able to 'be spontaneous' in today's education bureaucracy. If subtle jokes depend on seeing the other person's face, we couldn't joke on the telephone or the radio. How can the percentage of visual stimulus possibly be measured? Vision cannot be separated from the other senses, from memory and feeling and the way experience is mediated through language. And many groups of pedestrians—children, frail old people and other non–drivers—know about god–like motorists.

An English teacher, recently arrived from mainstream teaching, spoke about how very slow and complicated it is to teach Shakespeare to the year 11. Yet Shakespeare is an especially aural writer, reminding his listeners how his words have to replace the real thing and help them to conjure up scenes in their imagination which they have never seen. Two boys in the class spontaneously told me how they loved listening to tapes. Metim said, 'Wherever you stand in the wind, it is absolutely incredible, the way Shakespeare describes King Lear's emotions, the way he gets over the feelings and thoughts of this man.' Alex enjoyed the Iliad while travelling in Greece. Homer is said to have been blind, and it is interesting to notice how very seldom his epics refer to specifically visual experiences such as colour, and that is mainly in clichés.

Teachers reported serious problems in some families with young blind children, sometimes related to premature birth and lack of eye contact. 'Normal babies show they are excited when someone comes to pick them up, but blind children lie still and quiet because they are listening when someone comes towards them. Then they get very upset if they are picked up, unless their parents get into the habit of talking to them first, and parents who don't understand this get very upset too.' Families endure irregular sleep patterns when children do not know about darkness. Expert help with teaching language, visual concepts and communication is important, as is help with discouraging odd gait and mannerisms. Four blind young children are so disturbed that they are in a separate fulltime boarding 'opportunity group' at Louis Braille. 'There is no way that you can get them sorted out of all this ingrained awful behaviour, awful for them because they are screaming and screaming, very upset children. They need years of special treatment. Some have a very strong autistic pattern. They can't learn from other children because they can't see them.' This teacher's view overlooks the initiatives of sighted children, the many non–visual ways in which children communicate, and the (possibly adverse) ways in which these children isolated together will affect one another. The same questions about expertise arise as for other disabilities. Who are the experts, and do they include children and parents who learn through experience? Is expertise, including special teaching, mobility and life skills training, best provided and reinforced in the blind person's home and community or in a (probably distant) special centre?

Key differences with visual impairment include teaching braille and mobility skills to those who need them, relying much more on touch and sound, and devising ways of explaining mainly visual concepts. Older students at Louis Braille who go daily into ordinary schools and colleges show that these skills can be used in a range of settings. Parents are the main teachers during the first three most crucial learning years. Could skilled preventative help then at home to reduce the need for special centres later?

Almost all the West County interviewees changed schools during our study and were asked about their choices and changes. Five blind interviewees explain their decisions followed by accounts of five physically disabled students. The accounts vary in length because the length, detail and topics of each person's semi–structured interviews varied so much.

Selecting schools and visual impairment: which is the best place for me?

All the five interviewees are blind or can only perceive light or bright colour very faintly, if at all. They are all highly responsive to tone of voice and to cues which might be thought of as mainly visual, such as a faint smile to denote humour or irony, or the concentrated attention associated with eye contact. Their acute perception relates to main themes in the interviews about their abilities to gather and evaluate information about their education.

Susan: mixing options
Knowing that she could take up a place at Louis Braille, when she was four Susan chose to leave the infant school where she felt 'smothered and mothered. I had a helper and I had to stay in the secretary's office during break times.' She became a weekly boarder. 'Mum would have to drag me screaming down the [school] drive because I didn't want to go home! It was a new experience and I wanted to carry on. I still cry and get homesick sometimes. I probably always will.' Her parents say she has always been independent and has pressured herself. She insisted on learning to ride a bike like her three older brothers. She wants to be the first person in her family to go to university. Everyone in Susan's year 6 upper stream class seemed to be very happy to be with one another, with the class teacher and the demanding level of work. She likes the

after school activities; archery, Guides, judo, karate and yoga. She likes sharing a bedroom with other girls. 'We can all comfort each other. When there is a thunder storm, sometimes we get into bed with each other,' though she is sad when there are quarrels or thefts. Yet she feels 'stifled' by the very small class and boarding unit all in the enclosed school site. After six years she wanted a change.

When Susan was ten, she was interviewed the day after she had visited another VI boarding school to decide about her secondary education. She was confident and eloquent, and would firmly send other girls away if they tried to come into the room. She spoke of 'looking around' and 'seeing' the school, and she rejected it as too unfriendly and rigidly formal, and too far away to go home at weekends. Mainstream schools fairly near her home were beginning to include visually impaired students, but she and her parents thought that the staff did not seem to realise that as the only blind student she would need different kinds of support. They felt the academic level would not be high, and the schools were too far from her home for her to be able to have friends out of school. If she opted to leave Louis Braille entirely, they thought she might be forced to go to a local mainstream school by the LEA. Her father wrote a five page report about the options and the reasons for their choice, which the LEA approved.

Susan said, 'It's a really, really difficult decision,' but she and her parents thought she chose 'the best' by boarding at Louis Braille, and attending a local public school fulltime, sharing a fulltime liaison teacher with two other blind students. 'It would be a struggle but I would probably get the hang of it. I can take ten or eleven GCSEs there, and only eight or nine at the other schools. I could get maybe a better job... if I got really good marks I could get somewhere in life.' One year later, she was very pleased with her choice, academically and socially. She had made several friends, and not met with discrimination. Her parents were pleased about her integrated education 'she has to survive in a normal society'. Susan had another asset, a (sighted) friend at home and spent a lot of time with her. Her friend helped her to persuade her parents to let her become independent, going to the nearby shops and then on the bus to the town. Other boarders spoke of being very lonely and virtually imprisoned at home.

Richard: from junior to secondary special school
Richard always had poor sight and became blind when he was eight. His mother had many 'battles' with his primary school and LEA to try to get the extra help he needed. She felt it would be impossible for him to get an adequate education when he had no sight; the lack of resources and of interest from his

teachers felt overwhelming. They had a promotion video from Louis Braille, visited the school and were very impressed. They sadly decided to agree with Richard's choice to become a weekly boarder.

Interviewed at home when he was ten, Richard showed me his computer and a big lego model he had made of the Albert Hall guided by his parents' descriptions. He had changed his early ambition to be a theatrical lighting engineer to becoming a sound engineer. He performed very skilfully on his drum kit. Richard was extremely pleased with aspects of Louis Braille, his small class (the same as Susan's) and the class teacher, the quietness in contrast to the noisy mainstream class where he it found harder to follow the lessons, and the new opportunities. 'I've been skiing in Austria. I've done more at this school than I would have if I hadn't become blind. They encourage you to do all sorts of things.' Richard's mother was delighted with the academic support, the extra activities and the expert help with getting benefits and services. She was worried about his general welfare, the loss of his local friends and difficulties with mobility.

> He has a rather wild friend at school who is partially sighted and who will rush about dragging Richard after him. They can't use canes in the very large school campus and he is always knocking into things. He comes home black and blue. Some of the children have mental problems. It alarmed Richard when he first went and someone jumped on his back, it was a lot to cope with, being blind and away from home. But Richard is so optimistic about the unknown. He's been water skiing and he wants to do a parachute jump.

A year later, Richard was in year 7 at Louis Braille. Some of his former class had moved to the other VI boarding school, Susan and another boy went by day to a public school. His mother said that his class is now more mixed ability.

> Richard got the best SATs results in his class but he couldn't get into [the public] school because of his dyslexia. We've only just found that he has a reading age of seven. He was very sad to leave his junior class and his teacher and the junior school where he knows the layout. There is a lot of noise. They have to change rooms after every class, and he bumps into people who queue up outside and they get very cross. They [mobility officers] said they'd teach him body protection, to walk with his hand up palm forward in front of his face, but he doesn't want to look like that and he bangs into one after another in the queue.

Unusually, Richard is now allowed to use a folding cane in the school. The staff discourage canes earlier on, as one teacher said: 'We say they have got to learn to use their hands and to learn what they are touching, to build up an idea of the roughness of a wall and how the bricks are put together. They can become encapsulated in a little bubble with their stick, and not interact with much of the world at all. They need to be aware of their physical surrounds by feeling their way'. Other students were critical of the formal training plan, wanting to learn more so that they could be more mobile at a younger age, and not wanting to miss lessons while they do mobility training. Richard sounded sad and lonely during his second interview though he did not say that he was, and used phrases like 'it's not too bad'.

> The new class is quite noisy and you don't get to work that well, it's quite annoying, people being stupid and stuff... I go to bed at nine, which is terribly early. You can listen to headphones but you can't talk. I don't go to sleep till eleven. I do get a bit bored here.

He would like to play in a rock band and play an electric guitar, but the teachers organise only classical music and a little jazz. Richard plays the saxophone, and when he gets home each Friday he has a drum lesson which he loves. He is learning to use an electric typewriter but does not have the laptop eureka[1] which his friends at the public school have.

Alex: moving into mainstream
Alex's family moved to live near Louis Braille. He enjoys his family's social life, arguing with his brother a philosophy student, composing and playing in a local music group, and other out of school interests. When aged fourteen, he tried studying part time at a local boy's school without an assistant. 'One teacher there was very helpful, his son was blind, so he knew the problems and he made a great difference.' However, it was hard to arrange part time attendance, travelling miles during the day between schools to fit in lessons because the ordinary school could not offer him all subjects. So, disappointed, he returned to studying full time at Louis Braille, and believes part time integration cannot work. He thinks Louis Braille helps because

> it has a calm relaxed atmosphere and people can find their feet. In mainstream if you are stuck, you either manage or you fail, but at this

1   Eurekas are quiet computers, unlike noisy braille machines, which would not be accepted in mainstream classes. They can print out braille or printed copies, so teachers do not need to read braille. They are expensive and only older or mainstream students have them.

school if you do badly the teachers will help you. They'll discuss your problems because there is not the rush, the pressure. It's an understanding environment and it works for many students. But I've always wanted to be integrated. You [interviewer] can take it for granted that you would never be segregated. It's assumed you'd be in mainstream. For me, it's a privilege.

Interviewed when he was sixteen and seventeen, Alex spoke enthusiastically about his lessons, about politics, philosophy, religion, music and his ambitions. Like other students he said, 'I'm let down in exams because of the visual materials. My amanuensis did not know one diagram was of an electric circuit, so I didn't realise and couldn't answer all the questions, which I really knew well.' He thinks the school should negotiate fairer conditions with the GCSE boards for blind entrants. Alex criticised social aspects of Louis Braille. He had been bullied and said, 'In the mainstream school you could escape, but here you cannot. I feel very fortunate that I am not a boarder.' Louis Braille does not offer post–GCSE courses, so Alex decided to study A levels at a comprehensive school. Again he found difficulties with transport and access. 'A mobility officer came to give me some training about the site and my route from the taxi. But the taxi stops in another car park and it is hard to find the way to it. I hate to get anyone to provide assistance to get me to this taxi. If I'm late, it leaves without me.' However, Alex feels that he is doing well and looks forward to going to university.

Ann: mixing options

Ann attended mainstream school until she eventually lost all her sight when she was 14, 'it just went'. However, she felt that the main reason she had to leave mainstream school was 'the teachers' attitudes'. She disliked being at the special boarding school very far from home. She felt the staff were over–protective, and hated feeling that people pitied her. She longed to be more independent. She was sad to have lost contact with her friends at home: 'I sent them all birthday cards but not one of them sent me one.' Ann learnt braille with the complicated contractions very quickly, in six months, and she walked as confidently as if she had full sight. She took 10 GCSEs, and said Louis Braille was useful academically and to learn mobility. 'You don't feel part of it, but you just get on with it.' Ann began her first interview quite freely but quickly became constrained and seemed off–hand.

A year later, she was fluent and enthusiastic and apologised for her earlier response. Ann had decided to stay on the Louis Braille site, in the college for post–16 students. The college mainly provided residence, a resource centre for translating into braille and making tactile models, and staff who helped the students with homework and went with them to into local colleges. By day, Ann attended the local FE college which she enjoyed.

> I grew out of school long ago. There are lots more people at college, more freedom, you're treated totally differently. You're getting away from all this being in a special school. I want to mix with people my age and older, and have more choice who my friends are, not just people with special needs.

She had several friends including an attentive boy friend. She was taking A levels, and was very pleased with the college, academically and socially.

Metim: special school and college

Metim was a weekly boarder at Louis Braille from the age of five. He felt sad that this had isolated him from his family, he had no friends at home his age, and he was closer to some of the school staff than to his parents. 'I owe an enormous amount to the school, but it has certainly destroyed my relationship with my parents. It's dreadful that you can't talk to your own parents.' He especially liked the school librarian. 'If I didn't have her as a special friend I don't know where I'd be. I'd be unhappy, I'd be falling apart.' He had had periods of sadness at school but interviewed when he was fifteen he was happy and confident, jokey and full of topics to argue about.

Like Alex, he enthusiastically discussed politics, religion and literature and willingly talked to me for hours; his enjoyment of the lessons was linked to his liking and respect for the teachers. 'We have some of the best teachers in the country.' He criticised some aspects of the school. He was a member of the school council but felt it was useless because every change had to be agreed by the head teacher and she did not have time to meet with the council members. Later, the head teacher had the library moved away from the secondary school block into a huge noisy corridor. Like many people in the school, Metim was horrified because the library and librarian had been so central to the students' lives.

Everyone in his boarding unit was younger than he was, and he didn't like the 'constant badgering, nobody to talk to' and the lack of quiet and privacy. He mentioned that staff working in the school's resource centre on braille translations and tactile models said 92 per cent of their time was devoted to the few students supported in mainstream schools. Like Alex, he doubted the social benefits of integration into the nearby public school, believing that the blind students there were kept away from the others to work with their support teacher during the breaks. They did very well academically but Metim thought that his chances at a VI school were probably as good. After five years at the private school one girl went back to a VI boarding school to do A level, deciding that academically this was as good as the public school, and socially it was better. Metim talked about where he might do A levels.

Metim: I'm looking for an independent environment in which I can flourish as an individual and find out who I am... I find it very difficult to work out what I want, and what I prefer to do, because sometimes I feel like one thing, and sometimes I feel like something else. I'll decide and I won't budge. It's my life and I have to live with the decision. Basically I'll listen to my parents' advice and their opinions but in the end it'll be my decision.

Int: What if you have regrets?

Metim: Then it'll be my mistake. I'll learn from it. Each mistake teaches us something, unless we take no notice. It's part of being human.

Like Ann, Metim felt very differently a year later, but sad instead of happy. He had chosen to go to the college linked to the other VI school, which Susan had thought too unfriendly. Metim too felt it was an unfriendly rigid place and he had lost his confidence and optimism. He greatly regretted his choice. He had not done as well as he hoped in his GCSEs, and wondered if his former teachers had over–estimated his ability. He missed their warm personal interest. The A level work was hard and exhausting, but he had made a friend who was teaching him Turkish. He wished that he had been able to go to his local further education college.

They were very friendly and willing to help me, but they needed a year to prepare. I've got a tiny bedroom at home, nowhere to keep things, and braille copies are huge and if I pile everything on the floor I can't find it, I need space to store things properly. We could convert the loft but my parents can't afford that and the council won't help us.

Like Richard, Metim found the disadvantages of boarding were harder to bear when the benefits were less certain, but he said, 'I've made my decision and I must stick to it.' He talked about his longing to see, and to play football.

Eighteen months later, after our research ended, I contacted Metim and found another reversal. Shortly after his second interview he got an 'A' for an essay.

I desperately needed to get that, and I got back my confidence. Then I
began to do much better and now I have got good grades in my A
levels and I can do the very interesting course at the university I've
chosen. I'm very good at cooking and I'm pleased I've learnt to be so
independent. I play for a visually impaired cricket team and we play in
league matches, not very well but I feel a lot happier about sport now.
I'm going to take a year out and study for a term at a college in Turkey,
and then my friend has offered me work in his translation firm. So I
am still hoping to be an interpreter or a politician. I've been in touch
with Ann, and I think she's been very disappointed that she didn't get
the support and materials she needed at college. She's had dreadful
difficulties, having to wait for months and months to get her course
notes. So now I think it was the best thing, to go to the [VI] college
where we got enough technical support.

Changing views

Metim's changing views show the importance of assessing a school in terms
of its changing effectiveness for each individual in the short and long term.
Yet longer term benefit does not necessarily justify shorter term costs, or
sacrificing the childhood and teenage years for hoped–for adult gains. These
five interviewees were all unusual, as one of them said 'I'm an academic
person,' and they may be keener than many of their peers to put academic
above social interests. Even so, they all talked about valuing academic and
social aspects of life very highly. They were distressed when relationships
suffered for the sake of education—more so if the high price seemed not to be
justified by academic achievements. Some of them were concerned about less
able peers.

> Quite a lot of people at the school are intelligent. The problem is what
> happens to those who aren't so intelligent. Do they just get segregated
> into the slow lanes? Do we forget about them in the effort to better
> everyone else, and for the image of the school? I don't think we should.
> In a way they need more help than those who are intelligent. Are we
> trying to turn out hundreds of well educated intellectuals or are we
> trying to turn out adults who will improve society in the future? I think
> education is very important for helping people socially, teaching them
> to get on with each other.

Loneliness and undermined confidence are perhaps harder to bear when
mobility and hobbies such as watching television, playing computer games,

or going out with a friend, are restricted—they do have these interests but not to the extent many teenagers do. Four of the five were virtually imprisoned in the isolated school, and three were lonely at home. At mixed schools with sighted friends as Susan had at home they would not have been so confined by the rigid mobility training, which did not seem to have been planned in consultation with blind children and teenagers and did not teach them about their home neighbourhood. An education system which takes the students' views seriously would see academic and social interests as complementary, instead of inadvertently setting them in opposition.

Selecting schools and physical impairment

Scott: moving to special school
Scott has spina bifida and uses a wheelchair. He plays several instruments, breeds guinea pigs and likes watching wrestling. His parents battled to get him admitted to a local resourced primary school, but though it was purpose built, the staff refused to admit him 'and the special toilet was full of rubbish'. Scott enjoyed the first years at another resourced primary school, though it was an hour–long taxi ride away and his mother would have liked to have much more contact with the staff. The teachers were helpful, until he was seven, when he had an unkind teacher for two years. Scott said:

> We have to have newspaper for art, and she asked me why I didn't have the newspaper, and I told her I can't get across the room it's too crowded. Then she told me I should ask someone else to get it. I said I had already asked three people and they said 'get it yourself'. She and the welfare helper are always talking together about me, I know because they keep looking at me, and I don't like it.

The class teacher crucially influences the attitudes of the rest of the class. His mother, said:

> His teacher got this idea that because he has a shunt he's got, what is it, puppet syndrome? No, cocktail syndrome, empty talk where he doesn't know what he is saying or reading. But of course he knows. I was horrified. She kept saying she 'couldn't understand Scott', but everyone else can. [His welfare assistant] seemed to think it was acceptable for him to spend all his playtime in the loo with her. He takes longer than a normal nine– year–old but he's independent and can manage mostly himself and, poor kid, he didn't go out to play. Once I was at the school and they were playing rounders which Scott likes, but the assistant

kept him inside. He is a very good swimmer but he wasn't allowed on the bus with the other children, he had to go to a different swimming pool. It wasn't integration, it was segregation. It's honestly not disabled children that cause the problem, it's bureaucracy and nonsense and silly things that people do that causes the problems, not the disability.

The school spent money on a toilet for Scott, but not, it seems, on staff training about integration. His helper wanted Scott to wear small incontinence pads though he prefers large ones. With small pads, he often has to change his clothes, so his mother sent spare sets to school. One day his clothes needed changing twice, and instead of putting on the large pads to ensure that he would be all right, the assistant put on another small pad. When his clothes were wet again, to Scott's great distress she put him in a Father Christmas costume, as the only clothes available.

Scott moved into a class with 'an excellent teacher', but the family decided 'the damage had been done' and he must leave mainstream. His mother thought:

It was always on the cards that he would stay in mainstream and he could cope with it. But purely through the damage this one teacher did he had to leave. He was ill with stomach pains and terrible headaches and he wasn't putting it on. The doctor thought he had appendicitis and it was purely that he was in such an emotional state about school. All the other teachers were very nice, but I would never entertain putting another child through that. I heard how that teacher is still picking on other children with special needs. If he goes to mainstream, it's got to be done properly. The classroom should have been accessible to him. The teachers should be well educated in themselves and I don't mean academically. There should be none of that 'ask somebody', that's not acceptable.

It is the teachers I think that are the key. Their opinions make all the difference. It wasn't the other children that were the problem. Special needs children have enough battles. It takes him much more effort to get from A to B. I don't want him mollycoddled and we work extremely hard to make him as independent as possible. But having said that, you sometimes need to give a little bit of extra care. He began to say he wanted to go to a school where there are other kids in wheelchairs, which is something we've always fought against, but if that's what he wants, then he'll get our backing.

Since he changed schools, I can't speak highly enough of the change in him, it's absolutely amazing. His confidence has just blossomed.

Every remark I get from the school is totally positive, what a confident little boy he is. He's an absolute joy to have in the class, he's just so positive and he loves it. He phones up his friends in the evenings and he's learning Makaton[2] so he can talk to the ones who can't talk. Some students there take O and A levels and go to university and he'll have those same opportunities. Why should I want him to be in a class of twenty–eight, if he's got an equally good education in a class of nine? The extra attention and stimulation he'll get will get an awful lot more out of him. Yes, I think it will equip him at least as well as those other schools and in more positive ways.

Scott likes 'being with lots of other children in wheelchairs' and the school pool and, when asked, he cannot think of anything about the school he doesn't like. Scott's new teacher, Elaine, is very affectionate and she left mainstream teaching because she wanted more time for each child. She spends much time sorting out any emotional problems or quarrels with 'private chats'. The school brochure says that some pupils 'achieve impressive grades' in GCSE exams, but the staff plan to discontinue GCSE courses. Scott's parents do not seem to know that the cost of his present happiness may be much lower academic achievements later. Like the blind students, Scott is forced to choose between his current personal interests and his academic and perhaps longer term social interests.

What kind of friends will Scott have? His teacher Elaine said:

I am worried about the ones who survive and are paying the price for new medical rescue, life is a living hell for some of them, and what will it be like when they leave? Is it worse to be unaware like some of my children, or very aware like Stephen who is so intelligent, but in that body, he can't move a muscle. He said the one thing he wants to do is cuddle someone, but that is just what he can never do.

(Stephen, who appears later, is so attractive in his looks and personality that this view seems unduly pessimistic.) Elaine worries about the disturbed and extremely lonely children. When she worked during the evenings she found that they longed to have someone to listen to them.

Suddenly you would be surrounded by all these wheelchairs, because they are so desperate to talk and the care staff are so busy with their

2 Makaton and Bliss are symbol and sign languages used with people who have speech difficulties.

physical needs. A lot of our children don't make close friendships easily. They are upset about their disabilities and coming to terms with them, or they have just had a bad physio session. If they have a terminal illness like muscular dystrophy they know they are only going to get worse, and some of them ask what is the point of having this uncomfortable physio?

One little boy hated having to stand in frame so much, I started a feelings book with him and he would write 'I hated today, I want to die.' All the things maybe he couldn't say to his mum and dad. Sometimes he would write 'It's been really good today.' Sometimes it was so painful for him to stand, we took him into the physiotherapy room to do it.

When I came, so many children were taken out for physiotherapy I couldn't keep track of them, but now they have it in class. We have a crying need for a counsellor. A child will say to me, 'Why didn't they kill me? I want to be dead.' And I'm not trained to deal with that. And when other children die, they can't come to terms with that. A lot of them have to live away from home because they have this debilitating disease and they could die away from their mum and dad. I think it's a horrendous thing to come to terms with. Every third weekend the school closes except to the heaviest cases in terms of emotional and physical needs.

Ruth: boarding at junior special school

Of the ten children in Scott's new class, three have spina bifida and two have muscular dystrophy. One was injured in a traffic accident and walks and talks very slowly, and two others have serious brain damage. Two girls have severe cerebral palsy including Ruth who is noisy and expressive and has one word, the name of her doll. She uses a clip file with many pages of Bliss words. She can hardly use her hands except that she flips the pages quickly to the word she wants, while making impatient noises as if desperately wanting people to understand more detailed messages quickly, pointing to one word and longing for us to realise the rest of the sentence. She can read well. Sometimes she sticks her fingers down her throat and brings up fluid.

The staff tend to speak, move and work very slowly, taking time to collect the class together and settle them down before each event. During frequent group discussions, the children also often speak very slowly and ramble away from the set topics. They all introduced themselves to me, Ruth made noises, waved her arms, used her book a little and was interpreted by some of the others. Elaine is concerned, as quoted earlier, about 'the more able ones who are not working at the correct pace.' Yet with the generous staffing is it impossible to work at each child's pace? How much of Ruth's impatience is a response to her education rather than her disability?

The school has a gentle, slow, almost dreamy air; many students scarcely speak and some are lethargic from medication. The occasional protest or refusal is usually ignored or met by adults with gentle good humour. Paradoxically, this kindness can be a disadvantage to students who try to ask for higher standards, because it defuses or deadens protests more effectively than an angry response from the staff would. Many ordinary schools are at the unfortunate opposite extreme, with frequent forceful protests; yet over the past forty years, standards of teaching for the middle and lower ability bands have immensely improved, as shown by increasing successes in GCSEs and A–levels, and this is partly owed to the challenges presented by difficult classes who demand that teachers be interesting and clear. Some teachers at Douglas Bader taught in ways which no mainstream class would accept. From numerous examples, there is the reply to a nine–year–old who asked 'What's youth hostelling?' 'Well it's very minimal accommodation, but it's quite reasonable accommodation, it's a way for families to have a cheap holiday and though it's called youth hostelling you can be quite old when you go on it.' Vague, indirect answers in words which mean little to the student concerned were commonly heard. Teachers often said how little the children could understand and perhaps this perception discouraged them from attempting clearer replies, and then became self–fulfilling. One boy had several psychological assessments which stated that he was average for most subjects and a little below average for two. After he had been some weeks at Douglas Bader, his teacher said, 'He's not very able, a false idea of his ability has been created because the assistant at his mainstream school had done some of his work to help him to keep up.'

Ruth's class next went to a singing lesson and heard a tape of popular songs. The teacher chose one about a limousine and a beeping bubble car for the class to sing at the town festival. (Did they all want to stand on a public platform together and be compared with other junior classes?) At lunch I sat with Ruth and her helper who together told me that she doesn't like being a boarder and gets very lonely. She longs for Friday when she can go home to her grandparents. She kept pointing to 'unhappy, Thursday and Friday' and to her family's names. She enjoyed having a picnic and going shopping with her helper. She dislikes television and all the evening school activities, loud music and discos, and wearing a skirt. She kept making faces at her skirt and pointing to 'trousers'. The next lesson was about second world war propaganda. Then the class sat together while everyone commented on something good someone else had done, like working hard, being kind, or remembering to ask for the toilet, and they were given a sticker reward. Ruth wanted to show me her dormitory and I said I could stay until 4.20. We waited for our turn in the lift which takes only three people at a time in their chairs. A nurse introduced herself and we sat talking about Ruth's day, her plans for the evening and changing her into her trousers. Ruth was very excited to show me her clothes and toys, and very upset if the staff disagreed with her. Suddenly she waved her watch, to tell me that it was 4.20. A younger girl has a computerised Bliss board costing £8,500, bought with her birth injury compensation but which she is not yet able to use. As Ruth has had no compensation, she cannot have this equipment although it would transform her life. If she went into a mainstream school, the money saved could soon buy this equipment.

Linda: attending a 'special' mainstream school

Linda, aged eight, has spina bifida and enjoys brownies, swimming and riding. Interviewed at home, she showed me her bridesmaid dress with matching bows on her sticks ready to wear the next day. Linda lives near a resourced school and some of the staff are her neighbours and friends. 'Our caretaker Jim is married to my Brown Owl.' She has 'quite a lot of best friends,' and one lives next door. 'Everyone knows me. Every time they meet me everyone says hello and I say hello back. They just really like me because they are so friendly, the teachers are friendly and the helpers are friendly. I've got two half time helpers.' Linda explains how she is learning to do her own toilet care. She describes her resourced primary school as

> a special school, because my head teacher is really polite and she said, 'Yes, come in' [to our school], and every time I meet her she says hello to me. And it's a school for me and special children and other ordinary people who are all right with no problems. It's a special school because I've made lots of new friends there and I get lots of help with my work.

She looks forward to the new term. 'I feel I should go back and see my lovely teachers.' Linda plans that when she grows up she will get married and have two children called Kelly and Billy. She will drop them off at playschool and go to work as a hairdresser and beautician. Linda raised a main theme of this book: how much should disabled people be pressured to achieve as much as possible or be given extra protection and support?

Int: Is there anything else important about your life I haven't asked you?
Linda: If you want to do recorder, you try it. Because my teacher says you

can do recorder, you can do choir, you can play chess, you can do nature club.

Int: Is she saying, if you want to do something, do it?

Linda: Yes.

Int: Is that the way you want to live?

Linda: Yes, I'm going to learn it. Although it's quite hard I'm going to do it, to work hard.

Int: Is that because your teachers say 'come on, come on', or because you've got lots of go in you?

Linda: I've got a lot of go. [When things are hard] I don't give up. I try, but if it's too much I give up.

Int: That's interesting because lots of grownups find it hard to know when to try carrying on and when to give up.

Linda: Yes, my mummy's good about that.

Linda's mother once worked in a home for young disabled people and was impressed when a dynamic new nurse, 'a tornado' started to arrange outings and increase the residents' independence and communication. The family moved house to be near a mainstream school where the head teacher 'accepted Linda whether she was continent or not and she helped me to fight through the [LEA] minefields' to get Linda admitted.

It doesn't pay to have all handicapped children together, because they mimic one another. I wanted to give her a fair crack of the whip before she gets labelled as special school. She likes her school. They do call her names but she doesn't really think about what they're saying. She knows she's different but she's very outgoing. It helps that she's been with the same group since five, they just accept her and her sticks, and they help her, but with me she has to do a lot for herself. She's had it hard at home so when she's sixteen and out in that world it's not such a shock. Some parents do everything for them, and it is often so much quicker to say, 'I'll do it,' but you mustn't. It takes quite a lot of thinking out as to how much they [teachers] treat her the same or differently Her welfare assistants are very good and one does toilet and exercises with her from 11.30 to 12.00 every day to improve her muscle tone. She's very active and we often walk to school [nearly a mile]. There are five other children with a disability, and a physio sees them there. I think it would be awful if Linda had to use a wheelchair, a failure. It's harder for her to walk as she gets heavier and I have to watch her diet.

A year later, Linda was still enjoying school, and her new teacher, and getting muddy playing football and rugby. She got so hot and tired walking to school that she goes in a wheelchair. Her mother now thinks 'the wheelchair has got its uses. She can conserve her energy for other things and she likes it and uses it a lot at school.' Linda's and Scott's mothers spoke of their pessimism about their children's future job prospects, and this perhaps made them emphasise present social rather than future academic interests, though many parents of eight– to nine–year–olds would say the same. Linda's mother has begun looking at secondary schools.

Linda's mother: She is above average for English, but with her maths grades she won't get into grammar school. The girls' high school has so many stairs and I wonder how she will get around between lessons with a heavy bag. I don't want to put her there and then it is obviously unsuitable and she can't cope at state school. I would like to have a try of it, but I do fear that if it is too hard and she can't cope she will feel awful.

Int: Do you think schools have a responsibility to do all they can to make it work?

Linda's mother: Yes I do. If they are prepared to take disabled children they have got to take into account what's required for them. If they take her on, I will be quite honest with them about what I expect. I will have to go in and explain to them. I think she can strive to be similar to the others in a mainstream school. But some things hit her quite hard. She was in tears at sports day because she couldn't physically do the races, but then she didn't have the wheelchair, and I want to find out where she can play wheelchair sports, but there's nowhere near here. Her school is very good and they have realised their sporting activities need a bit more thought. I am very truthful with her in relation to her condition about what she can cope with at school and what she can't because it will affect her future. I just want her to be happy really. I don't like being told where she has to go to school. Everybody else gets a choice.

Jane: staying in mainstream

Jane is eleven, and has spina bifida with more difficulty with walking than Linda has. She was quiet and shy at first when interviewed at home, but has firm views. She attends the village school and values her independence feeling that at the playgroup 'they just fussed and made me feel different'. She has never been in a special group and does not want to be. The school put up rails for her but 'I didn't need them, I just get around like everyone else'. She likes her physiotherapist who visits the school once a month, but not her school helper. Jane and Scott both show the crucial importance of their classroom assistants.

> Jane: I did want her to help me, but I didn't want her fussing over me, that would drive me up the wall, though I have learned to put up with some fussing.
>
> Int: Does it make you feel cross or sad?
>
> Jane: Both really, but more or less cross... I felt very shy when I started school, and the teachers welcomed me and fussed over me at first, but it just wore off and I felt much freer. The head teacher is very nice.
>
> Int: Is there any bullying?
>
> Jane: No, not much. Not with me, but with the other disabled child who has hydrocephalus they kept calling her names. At first they stare at me, people who don't really know me still do. I went to the holiday play scheme and a little girl said 'how do you walk?' I said 'How do you think?' and she just walked away. I felt very guilty... When they ask questions like that I'm quite glad to be rude but after that I feel very guilty. I felt like saying, 'how do you talk?' There must be about twenty children have asked me 'how do you get like this, was you paralysed?' I just say 'I was born like it,' I just can't seem to get it into their heads.
>
> Int: Would it help if the adults talked to them?
>
> Jane: That would make me feel too different actually. I don't mind if they want to know but I don't want them to keep asking me because they can't get it into their heads.

The generally segregated system means that most children scarcely see disabled people. Jane's mother is also hurt, 'When people stare in the supermarket I feel like saying 'want a ticket?' Jane liked taking her dog for walks in the village where 'my friends were really close', but recently the family has moved to a beautiful but isolated house and she feels lonely and prefers school to weekends. At school she enjoys most lessons including PE and dance, she did not want to go on the school journey but likes the day trips very much, and being the narrator in school plays.

Jane looks forward to starting at the girls' high school. 'I didn't want to do the eleven–plus, mum said it wasn't worth it because I didn't really have the brain to do it, I'd be much happier at the high school and it's a lot nearer than the grammar schools.' Children from her primary school are moving on to nine different schools and none of Jane's friends will go to her school. Other girls in the village will do the twenty–minute journey on a school bus and she will go by taxi. The school has many stairs but has installed a toilet for Jane and arranged in the first year for all lessons to be held in nearby rooms.

Jane's mother described two–year 'epic' battles before primary and again before secondary school to gain access. The head teachers were 'more than pleased' but the LEA refused funding and the schools wouldn't take her without it 'so all three of us would not budge'.

Jane's mother: They kept telling us what was best for our daughter, though they'd never met her, but it was just to suit them. You have to fight or they'd walk all over you. You have to just put blinkers on and go for it and not budge at all. We've got the same right as every parent to pick the school we want. We've always believed with mixing in with all the other children, because she's going to have to grow up to be with everyone else and not have anything special laid on for her, though the doctor and the health visitor said she might want to be with other disabled children. If she doesn't accept the school and is unhappy and left out maybe we'd look and see [special schools] but she wanted to go to [ordinary] school. She looked round and gave it ten out of ten and thought it was absolutely brilliant. We let her make her mind up.

Jane: Yes, it was the best school.

Int: Jane, do you agree with your doctor and health visitor?

Jane: I don't know. I sort of agree that if I don't get on at the school I could go somewhere else but I don't really want to go to [special] school because there might be some children there who are worse off than me... I don't really like to have to struggle but I do like to have a go if someone can help me.

Int: As long as it's not too hard you prefer to push a bit?

Jane: Yes, yes.

Int: Might it be easier if someone else there used crutches?

Jane: Yes I think it probably would be helpful for someone else disabled to be there too because we would probably be friends, and know what life's about being disabled.

Jane went on to say that she looked forward to leaving school because some teachers 'do treat you like a little poodle'. She commented that 'it's bad luck for me I'm not normal like other children, but that's life', and added that she would not talk to her friends or parents about her feelings, but she would talk to someone who was disabled, 'no one else knows what it's like'.

One year later, Jane said that she enjoys school, the teachers are helpful, she has lots of friends, and feels happier and more confident than she was at primary school. Walking round the building is not a problem, and she likes the year common room where they can make hot drinks. She enjoys the lessons more, is in the middle set for science and maths and is very good at English and word processing and very pleased that she is learning so much. She wants to be a secretary or receptionist. The only other disabled girl in the school who is visually impaired is in Jane's class and they are best friends. Her main difficulty is with the helpers. After one term the first helper wrote a report saying the two disabled girls should be at special schools. 'My mum was very cross and she came up to the school at once and the helper left. I had another helper who helps with the toilet and with maths and science, she was fine but she had to leave because she got another job.' The next person to be appointed left before she met Jane, and then a fourth helper arrived who's 'a bit weird, she doesn't talk very much'.

Jane's mother is annoyed that when helpers are absent the school expect her to go in to care for Jane. 'If she has an accident they phone me to fetch her home and clean her up, they shouldn't expect me to do that, it's a long round trip. She wants Jane to take over more of her own care, be more independent, go out more and she is unhappy that Jane's best friend is disabled. Like many families in isolated houses, they have problems with transport even to go out to see friends. 'Jane's got real behaviour problems at home but not at school. We're in touch with the ASBAH (Association for Spina Bifida and Hydrocephalus) organiser. She suggested a psychologist Jane goes to see now. Her son was lonely in mainstream school and he went to a special school, he needed to be with other disabled people and we think Jane does too.' Jane said, 'I told you, I'm not leaving my school.' Her mother criticised the school for treating Jane differently, 'all the other children sit on the floor, she could too, but she has a chair. There's no reason to treat her different but they take no notice of what we say. The school don't know the problems, she turns on her happy side when she goes there. The ASBAH person told us about hydrocephalus, the symptoms, like violent mood swings, and Jane's got the typical problems.' Jane shows me an ASBAH leaflet appealing for £500,000 to build a unit where young people 'can learn to:

get up in the morning
decide what to wear
decide what to do that day
learn to make shopping lists

know when to pay bills
learn how to make appointments.
To our young people these can feel like mountains to climb.'

The fundraising leaflet exaggerates problems and implies that everyone with hydrocephalus has them and that they are all caused by the condition and not by social pressures or typical teenage lifestyles. Jane says she can do all those things except the last two which few twelve–year–olds do, and when she is a secretary she will do these other tasks well; she doesn't need to go to that centre to lean them. 'They want me to go to the special school so I can board and be out of their way.' As the special school will not teach Jane GCSE courses, she will lose the chance of becoming a secretary, without years of compensatory college education.

The classroom assistant seems to be crucial in determining Jane's choice of school. Assistants appear to be appointed to help her with maths and science (which they are not necessarily good at) and then told they have to help her with toileting which they may resent. For integration to work, the student and parents should be involved in selecting the assistant, and the job description to include teaching and encouraging independent self care be agreed. Assistants are low paid and usually pay for their own training. The LEA would economise by investing in better assistants to support integration.

Stephen: boarding at secondary special school
Stephen uses a wheelchair with a neck rest and a computer which includes a speech window on the screen so that he can communicate while he works on a programme. He works three switches with his chin, and he grimaces for 'no' and looks at the ceiling for 'yes'. He makes sounds and often has an animated smile. He types on his computer by pressing a bar with both hands, working along the alphabet until he gets to the right letter. It is very slow and when he has typed a message he often has to wait until someone notices it is there. Each lesson lasts an hour. Stephen began Friday by reading a GCSE exam paper with two short articles praising and condemning London, then he had to write an essay about London. He typed that he did not have time to read and remember the articles and write his essay in the lesson and he wanted to keep the paper over the weekend. The teacher said she could not give them out, it was the rule to lock them away outside the timed periods. Stephen typed 'I'm stuck'. The teacher said, do something else today, write about cities in the future free for wheelchairs.' He replied, 'I can't wait that long.' She answered, 'Think about it over the weekend but don't work all the time. I know you will think that I can't know what you are saying, but it will still help if you go on

thinking.' Stephen's computer went to be repaired during January and February and he had to do his course work entirely through making his yes or no signs. The next hour was maypole dancing in the hall. The teacher spent a long time sorting out ribbons and dancers and shouting out the steps. Stephen typed 'At this rate, one dance a lesson'. We laughed, and he was right. Although the group looked active, the dancers were mainly giggling staff while unsmiling teenagers in wheelchairs held the ribbons or watched. Then science, in an old out–building where damp had warped the cupboard's glass doors so they had to be removed. The lab doubled as a woodwork room and there was little equipment. The teacher said they must complete their exam projects by Monday. Someone arrived to take Stephen to physiotherapy and when he returned he sat for ten minutes before anyone noticed that he had typed 'in my bag' and then took his papers out of his bag for him. With a helper, he had designed small mazes for mice to go through, to see if they could learn their way and run through faster. As mice were not available, he had timed a hamster and was due to type up the experiment. After lunch there was an hour on computers with simple teaching games. The IT teacher said she had arrived five months ago and had 'still not sorted out all the chaos'. She told the class she hoped they were learning and not wasting time.

The final hour was science again. The cheerful teacher seemed to have no sense of urgency about finishing the projects, and walked around chatting. He said the rule was that he must not help them to answer their questions. However, some of the students did not even know what questions to ask, let alone how to answer them. Valerie could not think how to measure the trajectory of reflex responses to her knee hammer device covered with hard or spongy surfaces. Michelle had hoped to design an automatic door–opener, but did not know how to begin. Careful questioning could point them into helpful directions; without this they were expected to be virtually as inventive as Archimedes. Stephen seemed to be more scientific than the others, and able to remain humorous and enthusiastic despite countless obstacles. He spent the weekend at school, where the well intentioned staff could not give the care which parents and non–disabled friends together could give. For example, the school's stately entrance hall looks very welcoming and informal as it is often filled with the students. One rainy spring evening they were playing guitars and six small keyboards. Mark, aged eight, sat with his chair turned to the windows. An hour later he still sat with his back to everyone, crying unnoticed and unable to move his chair. 'Normal' activity and involvement is measured at very different levels in special and ordinary schools.

Therapy

Parents and teachers say an advantage of special schools is the on–site therapy though they also have reservations. Linda's mother, a nurse, thinks that thorough physiotherapy can be carried out daily by parents and children at home and that the helpers at Linda's ordinary school work well with the physiotherapist too. Linda attends hospital twice a year for tests but her mother wants to keep treatment to a minimum, 'I don't want her to have any more operations. She has to learn to walk again after each one.'

Scott too visits hospital twice a year and his mother refuses other interventions, believing this is partly why he does not get urinary infections which people with spina bifida tend to have frequently.

Scott's mother: I saw a television programme of a physiotherapist forcing a little boy with spina bifida to walk and I was absolutely horrified. They wouldn't have done that to a child of mine, it was horrendous, really damaging, and the sad thing was his parents felt they were doing the right thing. I was gobsmacked. I would have said, 'You'll stop right there.' When Scott was tiny he had one of those frames he was supposed to be in from morning to night, and at night he was supposed to have splints on his legs. I said to the paediatrician, 'You're not doing it, it verges on cruelty.' She went mad, but I said, 'He's not your child, he's mine.'

Int: What if they later said, he's damaged his liver and his kidneys and it's your fault? Did that cross your mind?

Scott's mother: Oh yes. It sounds really cruel but the quality of life was probably far more important than the quantity of it. He needed a good night's sleep.

Int: What if they said, preventing damage to organs means a better quality of life?

Scott's mother: I'd say 'prove it'. To be fair, I used the equipment a little bit but he was so uncomfortable, and he could hardly move, and he got much more exercise without it, climbing around. I wouldn't have had the guts to say no when I was eighteen, but years of fighting for special needs children toughened me up an awful lot, and working in a special school, seeing what it does to the children. A lot of decisions we made stemmed from seeing a girl with spina bifida on television and she was saying her life had been made hell by having so many operations that didn't work. I would never put Scott through that. He had one operation to straighten his foot, but after three months it went back again. We've been under pressure to have feet straightened but I always decline. If they could help him walk, or stand unaided or be more comfortable I wouldn't hesitate, but I won't agree to cosmetic surgery and have him cut just for the sake of it. He's a far too precious young man to take the risk of damaging him further.

I got a message that the school physios were thinking of trying these callipers. It wasn't till I said we've had them and they damaged his hip joints that they quickly took them away. The school nurse rang to say Scott had told her I thought his ankle was puffy and she said he should have it X–rayed. I said it's happened several times before and it clears up in a day or two. He can't feel much, and he doesn't walk on it so he wouldn't damage it. She said, 'Oh I never thought of that, I just thought you hadn't thought that maybe he should have it X–rayed.' I felt like saying, 'I'm not a fool, I know what he needs.'

Stephen's difficulties with completing his project were increased when he was taken for physiotherapy during science, after watching dancing for an hour. No one seemed to be responsible for working out a suitable timetable with him. Scott's teacher's earlier account illustrates how physiotherapists can disrupt learning and enforce treatment on resisting children. It is not known how effective most physiotherapy actually is. In the SLD school, staff spent much time putting on spinal jackets which orthopaedic surgeons say are useless (Theologis *et al.*, 1993). Students' lessons are more liable to be interrupted in special boarding schools staffed by therapists and nurses who put physical concerns first, than in ordinary schools where teachers and parents put academic and social interests first, and try to fit therapy around lessons.

The experience of physical impairment in East City: Siobhan and David

In East City, schools expand to accommodate for a broader range of needs. One secondary comprehensive has a signing cohort of deaf pupils and about six per cent of the pupils have a statement for learning or emotional difficulties. The head teacher reported that A to C grade passes at GCSE had doubled since the inclusion policy began, though this was from a low starting–point. Some staff believed that inclusive teaching (as opposed to coping with one–off placements) had increased their expertise in differentiating the curriculum during this period to the benefit of all their pupils. During observations it was noticeable that pupils asked for help indiscriminately from the hearing–specialist and the non–specialist classroom assistants, and that hearing pupils used occasional signs with each other.

Shaping attitudes

Siobhan started school in the same year as East City's inclusion policy began. Thus although she was supported by a growing political culture in the area, she was a guinea–pig at each stage of her school career. Her mother June had moved house into East City in order that Siobhan could attend a mainstream school:

> June: I couldn't get a nursery or a school to accept Siobhan ... They looked at me as if I was crazy ... And then I went to [an East City] school...and they said they would give it a go. So I had to travel, I moved here ... And it was like the people at [the town hall] who could understand what I was really feeling, which was nice because...[most other] people thought I was weird or I was mad, but they just thought I was normal. I remember saying this to my sister 'I can't believe this' and she said, 'Well, why not'?

June saw her main problems as other parents' attitudes. They were happy for their children to associate with Siobhan, but June felt they saw her as uncaring:

> They was saying, 'Oh, why haven't you put her into a special school?' ... People from Meadow View [special school] couldn't understand why—somebody said to me,'I don't think you've accepted your daughter's disability' and I said 'Well I live with it, of course I've accepted it.' So it was more harder for me to take Siobhan to mainstream than to special because I had people staring at me. But once they got to know me, all that was gone.

June kept going because

> as far as I was concerned, the children were accepting her. I think because she was in from the age of three, the children didn't have the hang–ups that the adults had, I think they found it easier and that made me more determined then to keep Siobhan at mainstream ... Things that the teachers or even me as a parent would be frightened to attempt for Siobhan, such as climbing on the frames, getting on the swings, they saw a way round it. And she'd manage to get up the top of the slide and there would be people around saying 'Oh God, no' but the children always saw a way round and got her down, where adults were frightened to master that part.

Siobhan's secondary school has now been fully adapted and admits some of the pupils from the now closed physically disabled school (others attend their local school). Siobhan had preceded them, however. What was it like when she first went there?

> Siobhan: Well that was hard work, because there weren't no lifts, and for the first year I was there lots of teachers had to come to me. First I had no lessons, I was sitting in reception and everything; some teachers came downstairs, some didn't, and I wasn't getting no lessons, but eventually a lift came in. [It was] kind of horrible, 'cos see I wasn't mixing with friends. First thing I had no friends, 'cos they was all going to their lessons, so it kind of built a barrier a bit, 'cos I could only go to lessons which were on the ground floor. In the end they were rescheduling the lessons, near the end of that year. When the lift was completed it was much better.

Did she ever feel like a guinea–pig? 'A bit, I suppose, sometimes, but I didn't mind. It was very frustrating not being able to get to my lessons though. That was the hard bit, not having the lift.' She says of the teachers after more impaired pupils arrived:

> It's all right, yeah. I think they know better how to treat them and speak to them. I suppose they wasn't really sure how to approach me and what to say, kind of, if they said something would they hurt my feelings ... talking down to you, would I understand. [Now] they talk to me more personal, suiting my age.

June says of the secondary school:

> I've been lucky really, I really have, because people once they get to know you ... I have had support, I mean I couldn't have done it without, you'll come across teachers who are quite supportive and you'll come across ones with different views who will think that Siobhan should have been at a special school, this going right back to the early beginning, but...there was a lot of difficulties at first because of classrooms and stuff like that, but once that was sorted out the teachers were very good and supportive towards me, towards Siobhan ... I feel Siobhan went back in that period, but she learnt a lot about herself also and about life as result. It was very tough, she had some name–calling as well, didn't you Siobhan, but that was just at the beginning ... they got used to Siobhan and stuff like that, and then it was fine, wasn't it?

She discusses the protective nature of the special school Siobhan would have attended before it closed:

Yeah, they can protect our children to a certain degree, but by teaching them about life sometimes we have to throw them in at the deep end. But that's only my opinion. And I felt that, yeah, it would be nice to protect Siobhan, I mean I'd love it as [her] mum, but that's not what I wanted. I wanted Siobhan to face the world as it was going to be.

In contrast to Siobhan, David started at Meadow View, East City's school for physically impaired pupils, and only moved to mainstream when it closed. He was interviewed when he was nine and attending an especially resourced primary school.

David compares his present school to the special one:

Like in Meadow View, you had no playground, like you had a hall, a dining–hall, just one big hall, it wasn't all that. You was sitting there eating dinner, you'd finish, and then you'd have to wait for everyone to finish and move their tables away and that's when you could have a playtime. You can't just like sort of walk out. So it was a bit different. In this school you can go out when you like. And I didn't really have friends there ... They were always teaching you the same thing over again, weren't they? ... you just had one thing that went right through the classes.

David says that the work is more demanding at his new school, and he has friends. But when asked for more concrete examples of the benefits of his new school he chooses to talk not about himself but Lorraine, a girl in his class who has learning difficulties and came from Meadow View. He and his non–disabled friends help her:

She was worse at Meadow View, she used to go 'da–da–da' for David and 'doy–doy–doy' for toilet, now she'll go 'da go da doilet' and you can understand what she's saying ... she's got a lot of more friends, and they go around with her—and before, at Meadow View, she had no friends, did she? She didn't even know no one, she just walked around on her own. They've learnt her how to talk and things. Kay–Leigh and them helped her ... They talk and she's talking as well.

Asked about physiotherapy and the value to him of these extra services, David says 'Why?', wanting to know where the question is leading and, perhaps, whether it is going to be a morbid question about his impairment. He steers the question back to Lorraine and his own withdrawal from PE, when he can choose able–bodied friends instead to go to the soft play room with him. His intervention in the interview process is followed by a description of how he has sought to intervene in his own curriculum planning:

> Lorraine can do PE a lot more than me ... I would quite like to go to PE some time, but I don't know whether they'll let me. I've said about it already. But they said they can't really organise a lot, because this is like, we just moved about five or six weeks ago didn't we, to the new classes, and we're still like sorting things out and what it'll involve ... I just asked them and that. They just said, 'yeah, we're trying to think of something'.

Physically disabled schools are catering for more pupils who also have emotional or learning difficulties. David's mother, Irene, had been a classroom assistant at Meadow View, and describes what it was like in its closing year:

> David used to come home and say like, they're not learning me to read or nothing, they don't learn me nothing there. But he couldn't see the situation...they were doing the best they could, because obviously they had other children to run around after and some were fitting, and if someone had a fit they couldn't leave them and say 'Well, you have your fit, I'm going to teach David to read.'

The interviewer asks whether the visible difference of David and Lorraine in a mainstream class is increased by the presence of classroom assistants:

Irene: Yeah, but they're not there all the time, they do join in with the other things that they do in the class. It's things like art and that, a lot of children with special needs are really good at that, and if it's playtime they go out and play with the other children, they're not with their support then, they break off, 'cos obviously the child would never get friends or anything ... They all join in, and you see able–bodied children pushing wheelchairs and talking to them and everything, it's really nice, it is. See, they don't sort of look down on them. They are close to them. It's sort of, 'Come on, we'll do this' or 'we'll do that.' All the other children are really helpful. They don't think 'Oh, I've got to do this,' they just do it ... Mahmood has fits, and the other kids, it's just one of them things for them, they don't take no notice.

Irene is now an assistant in the nursery at the inclusive school and remarks
on the changes on teaching staff and their attitudes:

> I think they're really good ... Nothing's too much trouble. They'll help
> you if you need help for lifting...and they muck in if necessary, if there's
> an accident or there's cleaning up to be done, I've never heard no one
> say 'I'm not doing this, I'm not doing that ... ' And when we need help
> with lifting or cleaning we ask for someone and sometimes we take
> one of the older children to help.

One of David's older sisters has the same disability as he has. Irene echoes
June's remarks:

> It's just one of them things, you take it in your stride really, don't you,
> you don't take any notice. It's like people all say to me 'Cor, don't you
> find it hard with Julie?' and I go, well I've done it since she was little,
> like just she's never gone away and you know, me other daughter helps
> me out a lot with David and helps me with Julie, and it's something
> you just do every day and don't really take any notice of it.

As we noted above, families and institutions such as schools which include
children with disabilities tend to expand their idea of the normal to include the
disabled member, rather than perceiving themselves as taking on some special
task.

Inclusive schools and hearing impairment

Most hearing impaired pupils in East City attend one mainstream combined
nursery and primary school and one mainstream secondary, although some
attend local schools by choice. Previously they attended regional schools, as
in most LEAs: a special nursery for the deaf, a primary school in another
borough, and finally a special secondary–age school in East City. The regional
arrangement was especially confusing for pupils because each school had a
different policy for communicating with deaf people. The new policy aims at
preserving and developing British sign language (BSL) and deaf culture within
the mainstream environment of resourced schools.

On the interviewer's arrival at River Road primary, the school secretary
tells how she has taken the Open University course 'Issues in Deafness', held
in the school, and is learning BSL. Like other East City staff she talks about
pupils in terms of the hardest case and of conversion. When Wayne first came,
a profoundly deaf child from a social services day nursery, his only

communication was to kick, bite and scratch. She remembers his fascination
with the fan in her office when he first arrived: this was their initial point of
contact, and he still asks her about it. She describes their conversation using
sign, and says she can't believe the change in him.

Each class with a hearing impaired cohort has a mainstream teacher and a
signer. A trained teacher of the deaf (statutorily required) spends about an
hour in each class every day. In a year 3 class, she is working with the four
deaf children at a separate table. Children queue up at the class teacher's desk
to ask questions or show their work and the signer, temporarily relieved of his
main duty, sits at a table of hearing children helping them and dispensing
rubbers and pencil–sharpeners. The head teacher was later to speak rather
defensively about the deaf children being withdrawn in a separate group. The
statutory requirement for a trained teacher of the deaf seems in this case to
determine actual forms of classroom organisation, separating disabled and
non–disabled pupils; nevertheless, pupils frequently cross these assumed
boundaries and re–establish contact. One of the deaf children constantly goes
over to the class teacher for approval, while a hearing girl several times
approaches the teacher of the deaf to show her work.

In the year 4 class there is a class teacher, a signer and a YTS trainee signer.
The class teacher discusses various books which she is holding up to the whole
class, with the signer sitting by her and signing to the whole class. Wayne and
another deaf boy sign to each other while the teacher talks. The class teacher
uses basic sign, duplicating the signer next to her; when she holds up the
books she continues to use the occasional sign for emphasis. She learned to
sign after the deaf pupils arrived at the school. She was a member of staff
before the deaf cohort arrived, and has adapted to the new environment. She
asks questions, using appropriate signs. Deaf and other children put their hands
up. There is an occasional noise from one of the former; no one takes any
notice. Then we start to work on separate tables, discussing how you would
draw a washing machine that looks like a house. The class teacher spends
some time with two deaf children on their own, while the facilitator sits at a
table entirely of hearing children. At another table hearing and deaf children
are working alongside each other, signing occasionally. At my table they decide
the chimney can be a packet of detergent. The girls jeer at the boys for not
knowing any brand–names; some discussion of sexism ensues, and a girl takes
the opportunity to complain about boys. As she says it she jabs her hand
horizontally under her chin, the BSL sign for 'boy', as an aggressive support
to her speech—she and the other children in this table are all hearing. There is
not a formal school policy of teaching sign to hearing children.

I ask if I can speak with a group of children in a quiet room. The teacher responsible has set it up very thoughtfully. The group includes two deaf children, Georgia and Martin, and two hearing children, Ravi and Patrick aged seven, who is Martin's brother. I am waiting for the signer, although Patrick does not realise this. He breaks the silence: 'I do signs so that my brother will understand.' He takes command of a situation, so that we can all get on with it; it is a demand for honesty that focuses on who we are, why we are here and how we are going to relate to each other. I ask them if they are going to bring food in for the harvest assembly. Patrick says he is going to bring in some soap, because the food is going to be given to the local homeless unit, and he says that people without homes don't get a chance to wash. Patrick is mature and dignified, he is respectful and not protective towards Martin.

Georgia, who is also visually impaired and wears glasses with a very thick central lens, seems rather vague about the significance of harvest (as one might in East City), but perks up when we establish that it has to do with singing songs. Georgia's signing is dramatic and vigorous, and she attempts to speak some of the words. She tells me about people sleeping on park benches, then the idea of bringing food leads to a discussion about her guinea–pig, who is particularly frightened of toys. The signer has arrived by now, and looks puzzled. Georgia explains that they are frightened of bright colours: she is eager to take command of the conversation.

I ask them what they like best at school. Ravi likes 'writing' and 'maths'. Georgia, who is his best friend in their year 4 class, finds this very funny, and has decided to liven things up. When I ask her she says, dramatically, 'Nothing. It's all *boring*.' (The italicised words are accompanied by sounds.) The facilitator pretends to be surprised. What, everything? 'School all *boring*.' Georgia says she wants to go to another school. Which one? 'Drama school'. Where is it? 'A long way away. A very very long way away.' So you don't like it here? Eventually she is laughing and signs 'Joke' (one fist on top of the other). What do you like about school, then? 'I like telling lies', and she laughs again. I ask her who the best signers are in her class. Ravi, who is hearing, admits to being not very good, but of course he is comparing himself with Georgia; although he is not comparing like with like he thinks he ought to be competing on an equal level. Finally we talk about girls and boys. Who does Georgia prefer? '*Boys*', in a very definite manner. She spontaneously starts to name some, finger–spelling: 'Manjinder, Michael, Andrew, Abdullah, Joseph, Wayne...' She seems to be struggling to remember any more. There is a pause; the timing is exquisite. '...Ravi.' Then she calls out '*Only joking*', with the sign.

During an interview at their home, Georgia's mother, Cathy, asks questions about the project and is demanding about getting answers she can connect with. She so much took inclusion for granted that when first asked if she would take part in an interview she said, 'I don't understand the words you're using ... What does inclusion mean?' Later she told me about a friend whose daughter is deaf and attends the regional special school. Her friend kept telling her to send Georgia there: 'It's a lovely school, apparently they got gardens and trees and squirrels and everything.' However, Cathy does not know exactly what a special school is, and does not realise that every child who goes there is deaf. Clearly an inclusive culture may just appear natural to those growing up within it, and this in itself may create a lack of knowledge about how the system outside works: a mirror image of the situation that applies in West County.

During the interview Georgia is very busy inside, outside, banging on the window, jumping on Cathy's lap for a cuddle, asking if she can do this or that, picking up the tape recorder as it's running, giggling into it and looking at the buttons. Cathy is very good-humoured about all this: 'Yeah, yeah, the man's talking to me, Georgy.' I ask her whether she was worried about Georgia going to an ordinary school:

> No, I prefer her to go to a normal school, because she plays with normal kids—not that she's not normal—she plays with her cousins, I don't treat her any different. And I mean, so I'd rather her mix with people who can talk, 'cos she's not quite, I mean she's partially deaf ... I don't think she'll be different to anybody else, 'cos the way she's got on, she's got on really well in this last couple of years. She's a good writer, a good reader, I mean her deafness might be an advantage, like helping other people in her situation or whatever. I mean she's not stupid neither, and she interferes and she butts in and she's good at—you know, it's where I don't treat her any different, and nobody else does, and I'd rather that, you know, than when they gloat on it, make more a fuss of them, then they get even worser.

It has sometimes been noted (Aspis, 1995) that physically impaired people may claim equality on grounds which might seem to discriminate against people with learning difficulties. Cathy qualifies her description of her daughter as deaf but not stupid as well as the difference between her and the 'profoundly deaf', and in so doing gives her view of how the concept of inclusion deals with the question of normalisation and difference:

Some of the kids at [Georgia's ordinary school] can't speak at all, but
I think it's better for them. Yeah, course it is ... I think 'cos you're deaf,
you're not stupid, so I think mixing with normal children is better for
them ... It's like with Down's syndrome, 'cos I know the more you fuss
over them and treat them any different, I mean I know they are different,
we all know that, but I think they should just treat them as normal kids
are, and I think they'll get on much better ... If you've got a Down's
syndrome kid I suppose they're not stupid, you'll be so used to them
you just don't treat them any different from what you are. And I've
never treated Georgia any different in my eyes.

Her description of Georgia's deafness as possibly 'an advantage' is matched
by the fact that Cathy has attended signing classes at the school herself, and
feels that she has learnt a lot in other ways too. Georgia's relationships with
others are couched in terms of what she can do for others. When I ask if she
makes friends with the other deaf children at River Road, the unexpected reply
is: 'Yeah, she don't leave them out or nothing.'

In Martin's family, signing is emphasised. In East City, where more than
half of the school population speak a language other than English at home, the
official policy is to treat BSL as a language in its own right, and Martin's
family have absorbed this:

Mother: I would always prefer somebody to communicate clearly,
    whichever language it is. I've never learned BSL before, so I've been
    learning with him. And Patrick as you know has been in the same
    school, which has been quite helpful ... But I had no problem at all
    with him using sign language as a second language or a first language,
    whichever is easier for him. We insisted on Patrick going to the same
    school first, so he could learn to sign, because we are all learning as a
    family, to help him if we can.

Father: The other thing we've noticed is that other kids who come
    here...with normal hearing, he knows that they're not hearing–impaired,
    so he'll make an effort to communicate, because they don't understand
    the sign language. So he'll try and use the voice.

Martin's parents echo Cathy's views on difference. Asked what their hopes
are for him when he grows up, they say:

Mother: I wouldn't say I've gone that far [laughs]. I just hope he'll be
    able to go through his education, maybe go to university or something,

and then choose what he wants to do.

Father: We haven't actually realised what his strengths are, at this stage ... Until they get to about fifth or sixth grade, you can't say they're going to veer in a certain direction ... It's the same for Patrick and Babatunde [the baby].

Mother: He's treated fairly normal ... I mean I know he's got the special side, you have to make an extra effort for him to understand, but as a child he's treated the same.

The family has expanded the normal experience of other people:

Mother: Patrick can be quite sensitive sometimes. If we go out and some friends or some boys they meet, they say 'Oh, your brother can't talk,' and he'll say, 'Yes he does,' or 'You can use sign language,' and he'll get them interested. They say 'How do you say this?' or 'How do you say that,' and he's quite happy to show it to them. Or if...they shout at Martin, he'll say, 'It's no good doing that, he can't hear you,' you know. He's got a defect, and he'll explain it quickly to anyone, so they can understand—which I think is quite good. He's always thinking, 'I have this thing to say, I have to accommodate the other kids as well,' and he thinks about how to sign it.

Some of their adult friends have learned some basic signs.

Father: Personally, I am for integration. Because that's the real world.

Mother: You live with disabled people all the time.

Father: There's no way a person who's disabled, be it physically disabled or whatever, is going to live with only disabled people ... There's equal opportunities employers and they still discriminate against disabled people, but slowly society is beginning to accept them, more and more each day. But there isn't any place that you're going to be working with disabled people only, well there are places right now, but I mean in future when these kids are adults I think there'll be a lot of places with people of all sorts.

We have already noted how frequently families who live with an impaired or disturbed child regard their life as normal. It seems possible that larger groups, such as schools, can similarly expand their idea of normality to include disability, thus reinforcing the families' viewpoint instead of doubting or dismissing it; schools can then be representative of their local community.

Chapter 6

WHAT IS SPECIAL ABOUT SPECIAL SCHOOLS?

Siobhan's mother: I wanted Siobhan to face the world as it is going to be.

Schools provide resources, offer certain protections to their students and help them to prepare for adult life. These three main roles reflect the conventional headings for reviewing all young people's interests: provision, protection and participation (United Nations, 1989). They also provide a framework for reviewing what is special about special schools. What do they offer which mainstream schools do not or cannot provide? The questions are considered in the light of the evidence we have presented in earlier chapters. The language of 'special' can distort all discussion about special schools, twisting it into pre–ordained conclusions that special means better and that the schools actually are special.

Special schools and extra provision: resources, services, expertise

Special school places cost more than mainstream ones and are better equipped.
Cost does not necessarily indicate value. Despite higher allowances per student, special schools have smaller total budgets, and lack the rich resources of larger mainstream schools: library and media, laboratory, technology, drama, arts, music and sports departments. Yet students with learning difficulties are likely to be in greater than average need of such resources. They are also likely to benefit more from this equipment when using it with ordinary students, and learning from and with them.

Every kind of disability is accommodated in a mainstream classroom somewhere in Britain. The extra equipment is not exclusive to special schools, such as ramps, lifts and low fitments for wheelchair users, and aids and technical support for students with visual and hearing impairments. New technologies increase the possibilities for support, for example, for blind students. When braille texts can be sent out by email from a remote centre, there is less need to bring students into the centre. The sensory room in one mainstream primary school is used mainly to calm disturbed children, rather than to relax already very passive profoundly impaired ones. In areas where all local children can attend their nearest school, or nearest resourced school, the numbers of disabled students can soon make the extra equipment cost effective. High special school costs, which do not directly benefit pupils, include transport, boarding fees, selection procedures and, in West County, maintaining schools in decaying country houses with extensive grounds. These costs can be used to better effect if transferred to inclusive schools.

Special schools have many more staff per pupil: specialist teachers, assistants, speech, occupational and physiotherapists and psychological support.
The main extra costs in special schools are for high staffing ratios. These do not necessarily benefit the students. In all the special schools we observed except one, some staff spend little time actually teaching. They ineffectually try to control misbehaviour, talk to each other, watch classes, or write records during contact time. The students spend much time 'playing', repeating very simple tasks, or waiting for small group or individual teaching sessions. The importance of the one–to–one approach, of small classes and special schools' ability to provide extra contact with homes have all been questioned in chapter 1. Paradoxically, in schools for learning difficulties, we saw pupils being taught much less than their more disabled peers in the ordinary schools we visited, and their resulting ignorance may be blamed on to student's limitations rather than the poverty of their schooling. Special schools do not all offer individual flexible tuition. Stacy illustrated the very narrow inflexible range which teachers at an SLD school and Douglas Bader school assumed they were confined to: she was seen as too bright for the former school and too impaired for the latter.

Special school staff stress the need to support students being integrated into mainstream schools; this can be of great benefit but too much support isolates rather than integrates the student. Staff time in mixed ability classes appears to be used most effectively in response to all the students, as in the class of deaf and hearing students (chapter 5), rather than being tied to specific students, except for the most profoundly impaired or disturbed.

Special schools tend to lack the range of widely experienced subject specialist teachers taken for granted in mainstream schools. Special school teachers do not necessarily have special needs expertise, experience or training; if they have special training, it may not be specific to their school specialty, and may have taken only a few hours. It is not clear precisely what special expertise means when ordinary teaching is assumed to include skills in helping students with learning and behaviour problems (McNamara and Moreton, 1993, 1995, 1997; Rudduck, 1996). Any extra special needs expertise is shown most clearly when special teachers and SENCOs advise and support mainstream teachers who have disabled or disturbed students. Their practical knowledge can benefit a wider range of students, by treating their minor sensory, communication or behaviour problems which otherwise might not be noticed, and preventing them from becoming severe. The knowledge contributed by students with difficulties and special teachers can help ordinary schools to become more humane and efficient. Extra staff and skills are especially needed in mainstream classes to help with disturbed students, and to resolve causes of behaviour problems; these are not addressed simply by excluding a few students.

Special schools may not have the relevant therapists, like EBD schools with no psychological or psychotherapeutic staff, and schools for speech and language difficulties with no speech therapist. In schools with therapists, the teachers may not coordinate with them to agree on the students' main problems, or on how teaching can be consistent with therapy, or on how brief therapy sessions can be reinforced throughout the week. Lack of coordination can raise serious problems for students, like Simon (chapter 5) who could not complete his GCSE project, partly because he had physiotherapy during science. Too many therapists in a school can divert the school's main remit away from education, so that learning is fitted around therapy and students risk being further disabled academically. Mainstream schools, with their firmer educational remit, are more likely to see that therapy is fitted around learning and that students doubly benefit.

Special schools and extra protection from stress, failure, bullying and isolation

Special schools do not necessarily provide more or better resources and expertise than ordinary schools. This puts greater emphasis on their role to protect students.

A haven from stress and failure
Special school students can learn at a slower pace, freed from the stresses of large classes, competitive exams and sports. Although special schools can offer supportive care, high staffing ratios intensely expose students to negative as well as positive teachers' attitudes. The all–pervasive scrutiny of the behaviour management system (chapter 2) was felt by some girls to be very stressful.

Some special schools are kind, gentle, leisurely places, but this may be at a very high cost eventually, and it is hard to achieve the best balance. Schools which are too undemanding can be boring and frustrating. Physically disabledstudents risk being over–protected, as if they are also emotionally and intellectually impaired, whether they are or not: staff 'fussing too much' as some students said. Self–esteem, which is solely nurtured through staff over–approval and token rewards, cannot compare with realistic self–confidence, and shatters when students leave the haven. Ben's mother thinks he is learning at his comprehensive school that 'there'll be no little groups to run to when you leave school... [people with epilepsy] have to struggle all their life'. His school is 'opening doors', so when he leaves, he can decide what he will do, 'he's doing his own thing, not expecting to live on benefits'. Schools which enter no one for GCSEs, 'in case they fail, the stress would be too much,' paradoxically ensure that everyone fails. If students leave school without the qualifications they are capable of gaining, they face stressfully unfulfilled futures, excluded from training, employment, social opportunities and the income and life style they might otherwise enjoy.

The concept of special schools as a refuge assumes that mainstream schools are inevitably stressful, or that a few students are too emotionally fragile to cope. The earlier points about improving mainstream schools to accommodate impaired students also apply to emotionally vulnerable ones: to encourage schools to be reasonably demanding and competitive, and also humane civilised places (Prendergast and Forrest, 1997); to see the most obviously disadvantaged students not as radically different but as the visible end of a wide spectrum of academic or personal abilities; to accept that helping them can also benefit a larger group of less obviously disadvantaged students, and can generally raise educational standards for everyone, academically and socially (Ainscow, 1993; OECD, 1994). Ben and Vishal (chapter 4) show how students who know that they are less able can still feel confident, satisfied with their work, and comfortable with their peers.

A refuge from isolation and bullying

A single student using a wheelchair or crutches in a school can feel very awkward. Linda and Jane were happy at their mainstream schools in West County, but Scott was unhappy. Douglas Bader school's proximity encouraged mainstream schools to refer rather than to accommodate disabled students. In inclusive LEAs, enough impaired students attend local schools in groups to prevent this sense of aloneness, and taunts and bullying about being disabled or disturbed are not serious problems or, if they are, there are practical ways of dealing with them. Pupils know they can talk to staff who will understand and act, partly through routine positive inclusive practices.

Separate schools are not seen as essential protections against taunts about poverty or ethnicity. Moves to open such schools would be seen as validating discrimination, and teaching students to accept apartheid. Separate schools for disabled and disturbed students powerfully imply that there is a cruel truth in teasing them, and that ordinary children should not have to mix with impaired ones. Humour and calm self-acceptance are better defences against taunts than segregation, and can deepen mutual respect and friendship between students. Michael in East City gave a typically confident example of living in the real world and not needing a haven. When Michael was Christmas shopping, a market trader asked his mother why he had a wheelchair, was something wrong with him. Michael replied, 'Wass he think? It's an early Christmas present?' Some rough play and teasing are accepted, and seen as signs of respect and acceptance by the East City families we interviewed, whereas the West County parents interviewed tend to be more protective and see their child as a victim.

Bullying is a problem in the special schools we observed. Students are referred to EBD schools because they are disturbed (victims) or disturbing (bullies), a volatile mixture. Some blind students at Louise Braille school are frequently bruised, partly inadvertently, because of school routines which can be avoided more easily in schools where most people are sighted.

The schools we observed weaken the arguments that special schools are necessarily better, and provide special resources and protections. The parlous state of some special schools suggests that they are used to protect mainstream staff and students from disabled and disturbed students, and as an excuse to keep down budgets in mainstream schools.

Special schools and participation

The rights of the child

This section looks forward to likely trends in the next century and to growing international influences like the Salamanca Statement (UNESCO, 1994) and the United Nations Convention on the Rights of the Child (1989). In ratifying the Convention, in 1991, the British government undertook to change national laws to accord with it. The Convention transcends national boundaries and professional territories; it accepts that education is for life and not just for schools, and that it shapes the future of all societies. The Convention sees children as contributing citizens. It affirms faith 'in the dignity and worth of the human person... to promote social progress and better standards of life in larger freedom'.

Children's rights are conditional on the child's best interests and evolving capacities, on the rights and duties of parents, on law, respect for the rights of others, and on public order, law and morals. Their rights include: rights to life and to education; to respect for the child's worth and dignity; the right to be heard; to prepare for responsible life in a free society; and to be respected without discrimination of any kind. Disabled children should be able to 'enjoy a full and decent life, in conditions which ensure dignity, promote self–reliance, and facilitate the child's active participation in the community'. While they have rights to special care and services, these must be given 'in a manner conducive to the child's achieving the fullest possible social integration and individual development'. This view has been repeated for years in policy reports, for example: 'Disabilities and significant difficulties do not diminish the right to equal access to, and participation in, society' (ILEA, 1985).

When special schools can provide a better academic education for disabled and disturbed students than mainsteam schools can, or a happier social education, then segregation might seem to observe the terms of the Convention (UN, 1989). Yet the problems remain that mainstream schools are allowed, even encouraged, to practise negative discrimination, to refuse to accept certain students, and to teach these attitudes to all their students by powerful example. Adults and future adults continue to assume that segregation is morally acceptable and possibly preferable; students learn to live separated by the glass wall (chapter 4) with no one to help them to reintegrate after they leave school. Reports that pupils have higher self–esteem or do better at special schools are meaningless if self–esteem depends on being in an unreal protected world, or if the school does not help them to gain the qualifications they could get at other schools. Many special school students will continue, as adults, to be unable to live the full life envisaged by the Convention.

'Participation' shares meanings with inclusion, whereas segregation denies the spirit of the Convention, the right of all children to learn to live together equally 'in the spirit of peace, dignity, tolerance, freedom, equality and solidarity'. Rather than the need for protective special schools, the Convention promotes humane, child–friendly schools for all children. In inclusive areas like East City, discrimination is seen as a social evil; respect and tolerance of difference are major concerns of social and moral education and everyday classroom practice. An example is the head teacher who 'comes down real heavy on them' if they pick on different pupils. Katsiyannis *et al.* (1995) propose allowing teachers to choose whether they will be involved in teaching inclusive classes, instead of assuming their cooperation. Forcing teachers into work they bitterly disagree with can only harm teachers and all their students. Yet surely their disagreement has to be seen as an extremely serious problem, especially in anyone influencing young people. Such attitudes urgently need to be discussed openly as the main topic in special needs in–service training, to see how non–discriminatory teaching can be achieved, with appropriate support and resources.

A strong argument against inclusion is concern that mainstream schools' academic standards will fall. Yet is not practical moral and spiritual education about justice and respect as important as academic subjects? Academic standards have risen since 1986 when the inclusion policy was introduced in East City. Examination success rates have risen, and the LEA was among the highest in the government's 1997 improvement league tables. It still has a long way to rise in the 'raw' league tables, which do not allow for LEAs like East City being among the poorest in the country, besides having many refugees and children whose first language is not English. Mainstream teachers we interviewed in West County who support segregation worry that they do not have enough time, skill or resources to make inclusion work. They assume their failure will hurt all their students. Participation is helpful here; seeing all pupils as potential contributors and problem solvers, instead of seeing the teacher as the solely responsible person coping with all their pupils' needs, ignorance and possibly hostility towards inclusion.

Repeatedly, adults in East City described how children led the way towards inclusion in personal friendships, general mutual support, and matter–of–fact acceptance of difference. Ben's father described how 'nasty vicious hard nuts' can be among the most helpful. Disabled children teach inclusion. Siobhan waited in her wheelchair on the ground floor for teachers to arrange access to their classes. Michael, Linda and Vishal say they have too many friends to name them all. In marked contrast to the vague repetitions at the SLD school Vishal would have attended if he lived in West County, his brother feels that Vishal's peers learn that disabled children 'in their own class' share the same feelings and experiences. He also said that having to find his way around his large comprehensive school increased Vishal's practical and symbolic knowledge which is caught through experience rather than taught. 'You get to know a vast number of children and see how other children are behaving, and like, the lessons are in different classrooms, they get to know their way around, and a sense of destination and everything.'

We are not saying that all pupils are the same. There are wide differences, but they are all part of a spectrum of physical, mental and emotional abilities. They cannot be polarised and there are no obvious cut–off points. They all share common qualities, needs and rights which far exceed any differences. Inclusive schools show that these differences need not matter. Differences can partly be due to physical reasons, but environment and relationships are critical in influencing how disabled or fulfilling a life each student can lead. The current main ways of defining and assessing difference are not appropriate, scientific or objective. Pupils are unnecessarily referred to special schools; a serious corollary is that other pupils with difficulties in mainstream schools do not get the help they need. It is more logical to assume, as the Warnock report proposed (DES, 1978), that special education should be a fully accepted part of mainstream schools. This will not happen as long as the option of referral to special school remains open, and the terms and spirit of the UN Convention (1989) are denied.

Policy

We certainly do not say that among the schools we observed inclusive schools are wholly good, and everyone is happy in them, or that special schools are wholly bad, and everyone is unhappy. We aim to present evidence which questions the widespread assumption that special schools are special, meaning inevitably better, and therefore that mainstream schools are worse and that it is unwise and unkind to send disabled and disturbed students to them.

We also aim to show how segregation to special schools can increase the very problems it is intended to resolve. It may help some students in the short term: some Louise Braille students achieve high academic standards but this is at the social cost of relative isolation from their neighbourhood and friends, and even their family for boarders. Some Douglas Bader and SLD school students feel nurtured and cherished, but this is at the academic cost of lower educational achievement than many could attain. Some of the small EBD unit students greatly appreciated being respected as a person. Yet all these schools exist in symbiosis with excluding schools which, by being able to reject certain students, are able to individualise and blame problems on to them. The alternative is that the mainstream schools look at structures in the schools which increase students' problems and which can be changed to benefit everyone in these schools.

Most special schools are for learning and behavioural difficulties and these were the most worrying among the schools we observed. If, as we believe, they were fairly typical of such schools around Britain, then widespread change is very urgently required. One step is for OFSTED to develop more efficient ways of assessing special schools. Another is to introduce more accurate reporting about these schools to LEA members, the media, the general public, and to parents and prospective parents at these schools. A third step is for LEAs to help parents to make more informed choices about schools, and to expand parental choice by opening many more inclusive school places.

Utopias and working for change

Inclusive LEAs might be dismissed as Utopias, unrealistic dreams of impractical, and actually unwanted, equality. Walzer (1985) distinguishes between two kinds of Utopia. The first is the dream of arrival at the perfect but unreachable endpoint, the land flowing with milk and honey. In the second, it is the journey which matters, the long effort through the wilderness while everyone changes. They never reach perfection but they do approach it in learning to live in new ways. This second, more realistic version accepts that 'the land would never be all it could be until the new inhabitants were all that they should be' (Walzer, 1985:101). This descriptions also fits with education as a journey, a process of change, and also fits with institutions like schools and LEAs which change and grow if they are not to atrophy. The former version of arrival is unrealistic, not only in dreaming of a perfect society, but also of one that will somehow exist even though its members remain unaltered.

In East City, while professionals tend to use the Utopian language of personal transformation and conversion, parents frequently talk in everyday terms that take inclusion for granted: they are not waiting for perfect plans or until everyone and everything is ready. Schools become ready when they start including pupils with difficulties and disabilities and see that it works.

Utopia is an optimistic concept but it can be pessimistic if it is seen as unachievable. It is only a short step from demands for perfection to despondent inertia. In East City, no detailed plans were enacted overnight. But although inclusion started in a small way, some fundamental principles and goals were publicly enunciated immediately: that separation leads to discrimination in later life, and that a disability or other difficulty should not disbar children from attending their local school. No riders ('where possible'; 'but what about—?') were involved; it was assumed that all children could benefit from being with their peers. The logical consequence of those principles was that special school closures would instigate and lead the process of inclusion. Several closures involved halfway stages whereby all the children within a 'special' category were allocated to an especially resourced mainstream school. This might be seen as ad hoc rather than planned, and as compromising the pristine principle, the students' right to attend their nearest school. Nevertheless, it was the deciding factor in enabling the closures to take place, and allowed or perhaps in some cases forced a change of attitude in mainstream. Most of the especially resourced facilities have since been phased out as younger impaired children have started to attend their local school. Parents in East City almost invariably cite equality first (in terms of peer relationships and social life) as the reason for inclusion; in many cases there have been clear academic advantages too.

We have described some children who were very unhappy in West County mainstream schools and happier after moving into special school. Concern for their suffering is often the strongest argument against integration. Yet it is a short term solution which does not address the real problem, discrimination, but increases it and makes it seem respectable and kind when it takes the official form of segregation. We did not meet anyone in East City integrated schools who would rather go to special school. Disabled children in an unwelcoming mainstream school can seem like David facing Goliath. East City schools show that when the LEA has a strong, principled policy, the Davids can help to transform unwelcoming situations without much harm to themselves. Planning, staff training and support and good use of resources are very important, but most of all a culture of inclusion is vital, among professionals, the public and politicians.

Special education: a matter for citizens

Informed public debate is urgently needed about the two main grounds for inclusion. One is the principles of justice and anti–discrimination (Christensen and Rizvi, 1996).The other is citizens' pragmatic self interest: many special and mainstream schools do not sufficiently help students with difficulties. In this, they do not give value for money, and they unnecessarily prepare many students for a dependent and excluded adult life and reduce their prospects of being contributing members of society. Inclusion involves change at every level: changing attitudes in schools and homes as inclusion is seen to work; putting support and resources into mixed classes; educating staff, teachers and also the crucial support staff, in disability awareness and advocacy; increasing the skills in responding to learning and behavioural difficulties which all teachers need; creating inclusive LEA policies to end the symbiosis of special and excluding schools.

Given the current extreme and unjust differences between LEA policies, integrated education based on informed public and professional support, proper transfer of adequate resources, and principled policies will only happen through a national programme. One course is to pass more clearly worded legislation without let–out clauses. Another is to learn from other countries. Over ten years in Spain, ten per cent of schools annually become integrated schools with better resources and staff rewards and higher status. There is a waiting list of schools for this voluntary programme in which re–education and rewards are likely to have positive and lasting effects. 'Where all children are included as equal partners in the school community, the benefits are felt by all. That is why we are committed to comprehensive and enforceable civil rights for disabled people. Our aspiration as a nation must be for all our people' (DfEE, 1997a:4).

Appendix 1

SCHOOLS IN THE STUDY

East City

3 secondary comprehensive schools, including 'Jacksons Lane'.
5 mainstream primary schools including 'Seymour' and 'Morley'

West County

Junior and secondary schools at a day and boarding school for visually impaired pupils aged 3 to 16/17. Total places: 130. 'Louis Braille School'.

Junior and secondary schools at a day and boarding school for physically impaired pupils, aged 7 to 16 with an attached unit for post–16 students. Total places: 89. 'Douglas Bader School'.

Junior, secondary and post–16 unit at a school for severe learning difficulties for ages 2 to 19. Total places: 90.

Junior and secondary at a school for speech and learning difficulties for pupils aged 5 to 16. Total places: 64.

Junior and secondary schools at a girls only EBD/MLD day and boarding school for pupils aged 8+ and with a post–16 unit. Total places: 72

Private boys' secondary school for pupils aged 11 to 16. Total places: 100.

Autistic unit for pupils aged 7 to 11. Total places: 18.

Unit originally for pupils aged 11 to 17 with health problems, but recently changed by the LEA into a pupil referral unit for excluded pupils, though still with a mixture of other difficulties. Total places: 24.

Appendix 2

FORMAL TAPED INTERVIEWS WITH STUDENTS INCLUDING SOME WITHOUT SPEECH WHOSE PARENTS WERE INTERVIEWED

Many other students, teachers and classroom assistants made informal contributions during our school observations. The ages given are those at the first interview

East City

Research name	Age	type of school	difficulty
		all mainstream primary or comprehensive secondary	
Alice	11		autism (SLD)
Barry	13		autism (MLD)
Ben	14		epilepsy and MLD
Chloe	13		Down's syndrome
Clara	4		PMLD
David	9		spinal muscular atrophy (uses wheelchair)
Sean	10		EBD
Georgia	8		deaf, partially sighted
Iqbal	11		non–specific MLD
Philip	12		EBD
John	12		non–specific MLD
Lauren	15		non–specific SLD
Martin	4		deaf
(with signing brother Patrick 8)			
Vishal	14		Down's syndrome
Rehanna	5		PMLD
Richard	14		fragile X (SLD)
Siobhan	16		spina bifida (uses wheelchair)
Tracey	14		non–specific SLD
Wayne	14		chronic medical needs, partially hearing

West County

Research name	Age	type of school	difficulty
Alex	16	VI then 16+ comprehensive	VI
Ann	16	VI boarder then FE college	VI
Elizabeth	15	EBD/MLD boarder	
George	14	SLD	epilepsy
Jane	11	local primary then secondary high	spina bifida
Katie	11	EBD/MLD boarder	epilepsy
Lesley	16	PH boarder then PH 16+ boarding and part time FE	spina bifida (uses wheelchair)
Linda	8	local primary	spina bifida (partly uses wheelchair)
Lucy	13	SpL/MLD then EBD/MLD	
Matthew	14	SLD	tuberous sclerosis, epilepsy
Metim	15	VI boarder then VI 16+ college	VI
Michelle	15	PH boarder then PH 16+ boarding and part time FE	cerebral palsy (uses wheelchair)
Nicholas	11	MLD then SLD	MLD
Richard	10	VI boarder	VI
Scott	9	resourced primary then PH school	spina bifida (uses wheelchair)
Susan	10	VI boarder with, from year 7, day integration into a public school	VI
Terry	15	SpL/MLD then part time FE	post traffic accident

Appendix 3

FORMAL TAPED INTERVIEWS WITH ADULTS

West County

12 mothers
5 fathers
4 school governors,
two of whom were also parents,

1 county councillor LEA member
1 LEA senior special education
adviser
2 education psychologists
3 head teachers
2 heads of special units
4 deputy head teachers
5 class teachers
2 classroom assistants

East City

16 mothers
10 fathers
4 school governors
all also appear under other
headings
1 councillor on LEA committee

1 senior education officer
1 educational psychologist
4 head teachers
1 special needs coordinator (SENCO)
1 deputy head teacher
1 support teacher
1 classroom assistant

BIBLIOGRAPHY

Adorno, T. *et al.* (1956) *The authoritarian personality*, New York: Harper.

Ainscow M., with Kerr T. and Norwich B. (1993) *Towards effective schools for all*, Stafford: National Association for Special Educational Needs.

Ainscow, M. (1995) 'Special needs through school improvement: school improvement through special needs' in Clark, C., Dyson, A. and Millward, A. (eds.) *Towards inclusive schools?* London: David Fulton.

Alderson, P. (1993) *Children's consent to surgery*, Buckingham: Open University Press.

Alderson, P. (1995) *Listening to Children: ethics and social research*, Barkingside: Barnardo's.

Alderson, P. (1998) 'Researching disturbed young people', in Hood, S., Mayall, B. and Oliver, S., *Critical issues in social research: power and prejudice*, Buckingham: Open University Press.

Alderson, P. and Goodey, C. (1996) 'Research with disabled pupils: how useful is child–centred ethics?', *Children and Society* 10: 106–116.

Alderson, P. and Goodey, C. (1998) 'Doctors, ethics and special education' in *Journal of Medical Ethics* 24 (1): 49–56.

Armstrong D. (1995) *Power and partnership in education*, London: Routledge.

Asch, S. (1956) 'Studies of independence and conformity', *Psychological Monographs* 70 (9).

Asperger, H. (1944) *Die autistischen Psychopathen im Kindesalter*, translation in Frith (1991).

Aspis S. (1995) 'People with learning difficulties', in *Disability arts in London*, 98: 4–6.

Audit Commission/HMI (1992) *Getting in on the act*, London: HMSO.

Ayers, H., Clarke, D. and Murray, A. (1995) *Perspectives on behaviour: a practical guide to effective interventions for teachers*, London: David Fulton.

Baker Miller, J. (1976) *Towards a new psychology of women*, Harmondsworth: Penguin.

Barton, L. and Tomlinson, S. (1981) *Special education: policy, practices and social issues*, London and New York: Harper.

Beane J. (1990) *Affect in the curriculum: towards democracy, dignity and diversity*, New York: Teacher College, Columbia University.

Berne E. (1966) *Games people play*, London: Deutsch.

Best A. (1991) *Teaching children with visual impairments*, Buckingham: Open University Press.

Bicknell J. (1988) 'The psychopathology of handicap' in Horobin, G. and May, D.(eds.) *Living with mental handicap*, London: Kingsley.

Booth, T. (1996) 'Changing views of research on integration: the inclusion of students with 'special needs' or participation for all?' in Sigston, A., Curran, P., Labram, A. and Wolfendale, S. (eds.) *Psychology in practice with young people, families and schools*, London: David Fulton.

Booth, T. and Statham, J. (1982/5) *The nature of special education*, Beckenham: Croom Helm.

Booth, T., Potts, P. and Swann, W. (1987) *Curricula for all*, Oxford: Blackwell.

Borthwick–Duffy, S., Palmer, D. and Lane, K. (1996) 'One size doesn't fit all: full inclusion and individual differences', *Journal of Behavioral Education*, 6 (3): 311–29.

Bowlby, J. (1951) *Maternal care and mental health*, Geneva: World Health Organisation.

Briggs, D. and Statham, J. (1985) 'The referral process', in Booth, T. and Statham, J. (eds.) op.cit.

Burt, C. (1925) *The young delinquent*, London: University of London Press.

Burt, C. (1937) *The backward child*, London: Hodder.

Bynoe, I. Oliver, M. and Barnes, C. (1991) *Equal rights for disabled people: the case for a new law*, London: Institute for Public Policy Research.

Canter, L. and Canter, M. (1976/1993) *Assertive discipline: step–by–step guidelines for effective classroom management*. Available from Behaviour Management Ltd., The Old Rectory, Iron Acton, Bristol BS17 1UQ.

Christensen, C. and Rizvi, F. (1996) *Disability: the dilemmas of education and justice*, Buckingham: Open University Press.

Clough, P. and Barton, L. (1995) *Making difficulties: research and the construction of special educational needs*, London: Paul Chapman.

Cooper, P. (1993) *Effective schools for disaffected students: integration and segregation*, London: Routledge.

Coopersmith, S. (1967) *Antecedents of self–esteem*, San Francisco: Freeman.

Cooter, R. (ed.) (1992) *In the name of the child: health and welfare 1880–1940*, London: Routledge.

Cornwall, J. (1997) *Access to learning for pupils with disabilities*, London: David Fulton.

Daniels, H., Hey, V., Leonard, D. and Smith, M. (1998) *Gender and special needs provision in mainstream school*, London: Institute of Education.

Davies, L. (1990) *Equity and efficiency? School management in an international context*, London: Falmer.

Department for Education and Employment (1997a) *Excellence for all children: meeting special educational needs*, London: HMSO.

Department for Education and Employment (1997b) *The SENCO guide*, London: HMSO.

Department of Education and Science (1978) *Report of the committee of enquiry into the education of handicapped children and young people (the Warnock report)*, London: HMSO.

Department of Education and Science (1989) *Discipline in school: report of the committee of enquiry chaired by Lord Elton*, London: HMSO.

Department of Health and Social Security (1979) *Report of the committee of enquiry into mental handicap nursing and care (the Jay report)*, London: HMSO.

Department of Health and Social Security (1989) *The children act*, London: HMSO.

Dessent, T. (1987) Making the ordinary school special, London: Falmer.
Dobash, R.P. and Dobash, R.E. (1986) The imprisonment of women, Oxford: Blackwell.
Dowling, C. (1982) The Cinderella complex: women's hidden fears of independence, Glasgow: Fontana.
Enderby, P. and Emerson, P. (1996) 'Speech and language therapy: does it work?' British Medical Journal, 312: 1655–58.
Fiske, S. and Taylor, S. (1984) Social cognition, New York: Random House.
Foucault, M. (1979) Discipline and punish, Harmondsworth: Penguin.
Frith, U. (1989) Autism: explaining the enigma, Oxford: Blackwell.
Frith, U. (ed.) (1991) Autism and Asperger's syndrome, Cambridge: Cambridge University Press.
Galloway, D., Armstrong, D. and Tomlinson, S. (1994) The assessment of special educational needs: whose problem? London: Longman.
Gardner, H. (1993) The unschooled mind: how children think and how schools should teach, London: Fontana.
Goffman, E. (1968) Asylum, Harmondsworth: Penguin.
Goddard, C. and Tester, G. (1996) Managing the code of practice: a whole school approach, London: David Fulton.
Goodey, C. 'Learning disabilities: the researcher's voyage to planet earth' in Hood, S., Mayall, B. and Oliver, S. (1998) Critical issues in social research: power and prejudice, Buckingham: Open University Press.
Gould, S.J. (1984) The mismeasure of man, Harmondsworth: Penguin.
Gross, J. (1993) Special educational needs in the primary school, Buckingham: Open University Press.
Hanko, G. (1989) 'After Elton: how to 'manage' disruption', British Journal of Special Education, 16 (4): 140–43.
Hart, S. (1996) Beyond special needs, London: Paul Chapman.
Hendrick, H. (1997) 'Construction and reconstructions of British childhood: an interpretive survey, 1800 to the present' in James, A. and Prout, A. Constructing and reconstructing childhood, London: Falmer (2nd ed.).
Highfield School, ed. Alderson, P. (1997) Changing our school: promoting positive behaviour, London: Institute of Education.
Hill, J. (1995) 'Entering the unknown: case study analysis in special schools', in Clough and Barton.
Hoghughi, M., Lyons, J., Muckley, A. and Swainston, M. (1992) Assessing problem children: issues and practice, London: Burne House.
Hornby, G., Atkinson, M. and Howard, J. (1997) Controversial issues in special education, London: David Fulton.
House of Commons Health Committee (1997) Child and adolescent mental health services, London: HMSO.
Hurt, J. (1979) Elementary schooling and the working classes 1860–1918, London: Routledge.

Inner London Education Authority (1985) *Educational opportunities for all (the Fish Report)*.

Jeffs, T. (1995) 'Children's rights in a new ERA?', in Franklin, B. (ed.) *The handbook of children's rights*, London: Routledge.

John, M. (1996) *Children in charge: the child's right to a fair hearing*. London: Kingsley.

Kanner, L. (1943) 'Autistic disturbance of affective contact', *Nervous Child*, 2: 217–50.

Katsiyannis, A., Conderman, G. and Franks, D. (1995) 'State practices on inclusion', *Remedial and Special Education*, 16(5): 279-287

Kelly, B. (1992) *Children inside: rhetoric and practice inside a locked unit for children*, London: Routledge.

Kuhn, T. (1977) *The essential tension: selected studies in scientific tradition and change*, Chicago: University of Chicago Press.

Laing, R. (1960) *The divided self: a study of sanity and madness*, London: Tavistock.

Lansdown, G. (1995) *Taking part*, London: Institute for Public Policy Research.

Lansdown, G. and Newell, P. (1994) *UK Agenda for children*, London: Children's Rights Development Unit.

Lawrenson, F. (1997) 'Runaway children: whose problem? A history of running away should be taken seriously', *British Medical Journal*, 314: 1064.

Levy, F. (1997) 'Attention deficit hyperactivity disorder', *British Medical Journal*, 315: 894–5.

Lewis, A. (1995) *Children's understanding of disability*, London: Routledge.

Lewis, A. (1995) *Primary special needs and the national curriculum*, London: Routledge.

Little, S. and Witek, J. (1996) 'Inclusion: considerations from social validity and functional outcome analysis', *Journal of Behavioral Education*, 6 (3): 283–91.

Lovey, J. (1992) *Teaching troubled and troublesome adolescents*, London: David Fulton.

Lukes, S. (1974) *Power: a radical view*, London: Macmillan.

MacIntyre, A. (1967) *A short history of ethics*, London: Routledge.

McNamara, S. and Moreton, G. (1993) *Teaching special needs*, London: David Fulton.

McNamara, S. and Moreton, G. (1995) *Changing behaviour: teaching children with emotional and behavioural difficulties in primary and secondary classrooms*, London: David Fulton.

McNamara, S. and Moreton, G. (1997) *Understanding differentiation: a teacher's guide*, London: David Fulton.

Madge, N. and Fassam, M. (1982) *Ask the children: experiences of physical disability in the school years*, London: Batsford.

Maras, P., Redmayne, T., with Hall, C., Braithwaite, D. and Prior, P. (1997) 'Helicopter children and butterfly brains', *Educational and Child Psychology* 14 (1): 7–9.

Marlowe, J. (1997) 'Cries and whispers: children are eager to show you their bleeding knees but not their broken hearts', *The Guardian*, 11.2.1997.

Mayall, B. (1994) *Negotiating health: primary school children at home and school*, London: Cassell.

Menzies–Lyth, I. (1988) *Containing anxiety in institutions*, London: Free Association Books.

Miller, A. (1985) *Thou shalt not be aware: society's betrayal of the child*, London: Pluto Press.

Mosley, J. (1993) *Turn your school round*, Wisbech: LDA.

Musgrave, F. (1984) *Youth and social order*, London: Routledge.

National Autistic Society (nd) *In your working life you can expect to meet several people with autism: will you recognise them?* London: NAS.

National Children's Bureau (1996), conference reported in *The Guardian*, 10.7.96.

National Curriculum Council (1993) *Special needs and the national curriculum*, York: NCC.

National Curriculum Council (1993) *Spiritual and moral development: a discussion paper*, York: NCC.

Norwich, B. (1994) 'Differentiation: from the perspective of resolving tensions between basic social values and assumptions about individual differences', *Curriculum Studies* 2 (3): 289–308.

Norwich, B. (1994) *Segregation and inclusion: English LEA statistics*, Bristol: Centre for Studies in Inclusive Education.

Norwich, B. (1996) *Special needs education, inclusive education or just education for all?* London: Institute of Education.

OECD (1994) *The integration of special children into mainstream education: ambitions, theories and practices*, Paris: OECD.

Oliver, M. (1996) *Understanding disability: from theory to practice*, Basingstoke: Macmillan.

Oswin, M. (1971) *The empty hours*, Harmondsworth: Penguin.

Pailthorpe, G. (1932) *Studies in psychology of delinquency*, London: HMSO.

Penn, H. (1997) *Comparing nurseries*, London: Paul Chapman.

Potts, P. and Statham, J. (1982/5) 'Off–duty: educational psychologists discuss their job', in Booth, T. and Statham, J. (eds.) op. cit.

Prendergast, S. and Forrest, S. (1997) 'Shorties, low lifers, hard nuts and kings: embodiment and emotions in school' in Bendelow, G. and Williams, S. (eds.) *Emotions in social life: social theories and contemporary issues*, London: Routledge.

Quicke, J., Beasley, K. and Morrison, C. (1990) *Challenging prejudice through education*, London: Falmer.

Rudduck, J. (1996), *Making your way through secondary school*, Buckingham: Open University Press.

Sammons, P., Hillman, M. and Mortimore, P. (1995) *Key characteristics of effective schools*, London: Office for Standards in Education.

Seligman, M. (1975) *Helplessness: on depression, development and death*, San Francisco: Freeman.

Sherif, M. (1966) *Group conflict and co-operation: their social psychology*, London: Routledge.

Smith, P. and Sharp, S. (1994) *School bullying: insights*, London: Routledge.

Stoll, L. and Fink, D (1996) *Changing our schools*, Buckingham: Open University Press.

Tattum, E. and Tattum, D. (1992) *Social education and personal development*, London: David Fulton.

Theologis, T. *et al.* (1993) 'Quantifying the cosmetic defect of adolescent ideopathic scoliosis', *Spine* 18: 909–12.

Tizzard, B. and Hughes, M. (1984) *Young children learning*, London: Fontana.

Tomlinson, S. (1982) *A sociology of special needs*, London: Routledge.

UNESCO. (1994) *Declaration of world conference on special educational needs (the Salamanca declaration)*, Paris: UNESCO.

United Nations. (1989) *Convention on the rights of the child*, Geneva: UN.

Voysey, M. (1975) *A constant burden*, London: Routledge.

Wade, B. and Moore, M. (1992) *Experiencing special education: what young people with special educational needs can tell us*, Buckingham: Open University Press.

Walzer, M. (1985) *Exodus and revolution*, New York: Basic Books.

Wedell, K. (1995) 'Making inclusive education ordinary', *British Journal of Special Education* 22 (3): 100–4.

Wedell, K. (1993) *Special needs education: the next 25 years*, London: National Commission on Education.

Whitaker, J. (1991) 'Three surprising ways of impeding the integration of students with special needs into FE curricular contexts', *Vocational Aspects of Education* 43 (3): 225–229.

Wilkinson, R. (1994) *Unfair shares*, Barkingside: Barnardo's.

Wing, L. (1981) 'Language, social and cognitive impairments in autism and severe mental retardation', *Journal of Autism and Development Disorders*, 11: 31–44.

Wing, L. (1997) 'The history of ideas on autism: legends, myth and reality', *Autism*, 1 (1) 13–24.

Wright, S. (1997) 'A little understood solution to a vaguely defined problem: parental perceptions of Ritalin', *Educational and Child Psychology* 14 (1): 50–59.

Zimbardo, P., Banks, W., Craig, H. and Jaffe, D. (1973) *A Pirandellian prison*, New York: New York Times Magazine, 8 April: 38–60.